HUMAN RIGHTS IN CUBA

The Need to Sustain the Pressure

An Americas Watch Report

January 1989

36 W. 44th Street   1522 K Street, NW, #910
New York, NY 10036   Washington, DC 20005
212-840-9460   202-371-6592

Cover design by Charlotte Staub

Table of Contents

ACKNOWLEDGMENTS

This report was written by Mary Jane Camejo, Americas Watch Research Associate, and is based in part on information gathered in Cuba by several members of the Board and staff of Americas Watch who visited during 1988 in addition to Ms. Camejo. Since Americas Watch itself was not permitted to send a mission to Cuba, representatives of Americas Watch travelled under the auspices of other groups, though Cuban authorities were made aware of their affiliation with Americas Watch.

Americas Watch expresses gratitude to the Cuban Committee for Human Rights and the Cuban Commission for Human Rights and National Reconciliation for the information that they helped us to obtain during our visits to Cuba and in regular telephone contact throughout the past year. Americas Watch is also very grateful to many Cubans living in the U.S. who provided us with invaluable assistance.

INTRODUCTION

Ironically, the question of abuses of human rights in Cuba has attracted attention in recent years primarily as a consequence of the releases of political prisoners. In the 1980s, prisoners who had served sentences of twenty years or more since the early period following the Cuban revolution completed their sentences and were released. After they got out of prison and, in many cases, left the country, they informed the world about their comrades who remained in prison and about the conditions of confinement that they had endured. Not surprisingly, therefore, the main focus of international concern with respect to human rights in Cuba has been on these questions of political imprisonment and prison conditions.

Americas Watch contributed to the concern with these issues by publishing in April 1986 Jorge Valls's memoir of his imprisonment, *Twenty Years and Forty Days*. Though the publication of such a document is not characteristic of our work, we made an exception in this case for two reasons: first, we had been barred by the Cuban government from conducting the kind of investigation that we have undertaken elsewhere and, therefore, were then unable to issue a report such as we had published on other countries; and, second, we thought that publishing Valls's memoir was of intrinsic importance and would contribute to knowledge about human rights in Cuba.

In the nearly three years that have elapsed since we published the Valls memoir, a number of things have changed. To a significant degree, the international attention that has been focused on political prisoners and on the conditions of confinement has had a positive impact. That does not mean that all the political prisoners have been released; they have not. Though the Castro government has now promised to release all, or almost all, those convicted for what it considers to be political crimes, at least several score additional Cubans, and possibly as many as a few hundred, remain in prison for non-violent offenses on

1

charges such as *salida ilegal* (illegal exit) for trying to leave the country without permission which has been arbitrarily denied to them; or *desacato* (contempt) for speaking disrespectfully about Fidel Castro or other high officials; and *clandestinidad de impresos* (clandestine printing) under which Jehovah's Witnesses are among those who have been imprisoned. In addition, an unknown number of conscientious objectors remain in Cuba's military prisons. Unlike the civilian prisons which have been opened to many outsiders in the last couple of years, the military prisons remain off limits and it is impossible for us even to speculate as to how many conscientious objectors might be confined. Military service is compulsory in Cuba and there is no provision for alternative service. Americas Watch believes that governments should provide opportunities for alternative service to those whose refusal to perform military service is grounded on reasons of conscience. Failing this they should not be imprisoned.

As far as the conditions of confinement are concerned, the Cuban government has attempted to refute the reports of former political prisoners by opening its prisons to international inspection. Several persons associated with Americas Watch have taken part in such inspections conducted by other organizations. It has been evident to us that many abusive conditions have been corrected. Some may have been corrected for the sole purpose of presenting a more pleasing picture to us and to other visitors. Other abuses have not been corrected, however, and we have seen some conditions that are cruel, inhuman and degrading though we believe that, if international inspections can be sustained, it will be necessary for the Cuban authorities to make further changes so as to avoid the embarrassment caused by reports on these conditions.

Though political imprisonment and the conditions of confinement are discussed in this report, they are not our main focus. One reason is that the reduction in abuses in these areas makes it possible to devote attention to other issues. Another reason is that, though Americas Watch has still not itself obtained permission to visit Cuba, the fact that a number of persons connected to Americas Watch were permitted to visit under other auspices has aided us in gathering information on other aspects of the human rights situation in Cuba. But the most important reason is that the issues on which this report focuses are on-going and serious violations of human rights that victimize the whole Cuban population.

The rights with which this report is principally concerned are freedom of expression, freedom of association, freedom of assembly, freedom of movement, the right to privacy and due process of law. These rights are denied systematically in both law and practice.

The Cuban Constitution itself denies freedom of expression by specifying that speech and press are protected only to the degree that what is spoken or published is "in keeping with the objectives of socialist society" and that none of the freedoms afforded to Cuban citizens may be "exercised against ... the objectives of the socialist State, nor against the decision of the Cuban people to build socialism and communism." These and other constitutional provisions are implemented by laws and practices that place all the media of communications in the hands of the government and that penalize a broad range of expression as "enemy propaganda," "contempt" or "public disorder."

Freedom of association and assembly are denied by provisions of Cuban law that penalize "illicit associations, gatherings and demonstrations." Associations that are not registered are considered illicit as are gatherings or demonstrations that are not authorized. Only those associations, gatherings or demonstrations that are considered by the government to be in keeping with "the objectives of socialist society" are accorded the necessary official recognition.

Of all rights, the most systematically violated in Cuba is the right to privacy. Almost every aspect of the lives of Cubans is subject to a pervasive system of political surveillance so that Cubans are monitored in their neighborhoods, at their places of work and in their schools. Their degree of "ideological integration" is constantly being recorded and their lives are shaped by judgments about how their conduct and their views conform to officially prescribed doctrines.

Cubans are not free to leave their country, or to leave and return without being subjected to a certain amount of harassment. Attempts to leave without permission are severely punished. Of the remaining political prisoners

3

and of the continuing political detentions, a large proportion involve what are considered under Cuban law to be illegal attempts to leave the country.

Due process of law is denied to Cubans because the courts are, according to the Constitution, subordinate to the other branches of government and have among their main objectives "to uphold and strengthen socialist legality." Many of the judges are Communist Party members under Party discipline and all of them are required to have "active revolutionary integration." Cuban lawyers are required to practice their profession as members of collectives and the national organization of collectives has made it clear that it is their duty to place "the victory of the law and the humanist principles of our justice" ahead of the interests of their clients. In practice this means that Cuban lawyers often do not defend their clients vigorously in trials involving politically motivated offenses.

Like other countries, but to a lesser degree than many, Cuba has been afflicted by AIDS. Unlike other countries, Cuba has reacted by subjecting its entire population to mandatory testing and by depriving of liberty all those who test positive. The treatment of those testing positive is one indication of the balance that is struck in Cuba between the interest in security and the interest in liberty; that is, liberty is given no weight at all.

In attempting to focus attention on denials of freedom of expression, freedom of association, freedom of assembly, freedom of movement, the right to privacy and due process of law, Americas Watch is mindful that these issues, serious as they are, may not seem of overriding significance given the charges that have been made by the U.S. government that Cuba engages in torture, disappearances and political executions and continues to hold 10,000 or 15,000 or more political prisoners. We regret that such charges have been made by our government. In our view, there is no evidence that these abuses were practiced in the last year or two, when the allegations were made. Given the lack of evidence to back up such charges, we consider that bringing them is irresponsible. Moreover, we are concerned that, because such charges are so sensational, they will obscure the significance of the severe denials of human rights to which Cubans are in fact subjected.

4

A particular concern of Americas Watch at this time involves consideration of the Cuban case by the United Nations Commission on Human Rights. Largely as a consequence of the efforts of the United States, the Cuban case has been taken up by the U.N. In March 1988, Cuba avoided the possibility that the U.N. Commission would vote to condemn abuses of human rights in Cuba by inviting a U.N. delegation to visit. The U.N. delegation visited in September 1988 and is expected to report its findings shortly. Our concern is that, because the U.N. delegation probably did not find evidence to validate the sensational charges by the United States, its report may appear to give Cuba a clean bill of health.

Any such result would be very unfortunate. Cuba's success in refuting exaggerated charges should not be the measure of its human rights record. As we attempt to make clear in this report, Cuba's human rights practices are sharply at odds with international standards and the record should be judged according to those standards, not according to the charges by the United States.

Moreover, we are concerned that failure to sustain U.N. scrutiny of Cuba's human rights record would send the wrong signal. The fact that Cuba's human rights practices have at last attracted international attention in recent years has resulted in the mitigation of some abuses. Equally significant, it has provided some space that has permitted the beginnings of a civil society to emerge. By keeping the spotlight on Cuba, the United Nations Commission on Human Rights could exert a positive influence and could help to make it possible for that civil society to grow and to blossom.

It is the hope of Americas Watch that, in publishing this report, we will make a contribution to the process of maintaining international attention on the human rights situation in Cuba and, thereby, to the further reduction of abuses of human rights.

FREEDOM OF EXPRESSION

Cuban law limits the expression of opinion, ideas and information to that which conforms to official ideology. The free expression provisions of the Cuban Constitution do not guarantee the exercise of freedom of expression by groups that are unofficial and independent of the government. Article 52 of the Constitution protects only speech and press freedom which is "in keeping with the objectives of socialist society. "Article 38(e) provides that "artistic creativity is free as long as its content is not contrary to the Revolution." These vague provisions are, of course, susceptible to arbitrary interpretation.

Accordingly, Cuban law falls short of the internationally accepted standards embodied in Article 19 of the Universal Declaration of Human Rights which states that "Everyone has the right to freedom of opinion and expression; this right includes freedom to hold opinions without interference and to seek, receive and impart information and ideas through any media and regardless of frontiers."

Article 52, also states that "the press, radio, television, movies and other organs of the mass media are state or social property," thereby providing for "their use at the exclusive service of the working people and in the interest of society." In order to broadcast, publish, perform, or exhibit, Cubans must belong to an official "social and mass organization," such as the writers' and artists' union or the radio and television or film institutes. Government control of all media precludes opposition speech or press, especially in light of Article 61 which states that none of the freedoms afforded Cuban citizens may be "exercised against... the existence and objectives of the socialist State, nor against the decision of the Cuban people to build socialism and communism. Infraction of this principle is punishable. "Far from guaranteeing the right of individual Cubans to speak or to publish and disseminate writings that diverge from the government's position, Cuba's fundamental law is a prohibition on dissent.

Although Article 291 of the current penal code makes it a crime punishable by three months to one year in prison to "impede the exercise of the right of freedom of speech or press guaranteed by the Constitution," and by six months to two years in prison if this crime is committed by a public official, Americas Watch knows of no prosecutions or convictions on this charge.[1] In any case, the fact remains that the freedom of speech guaranteed by the Constitution is limited to that which does not offend the government.

Since 1986, when Cuba's human rights practices came under increasingly close scrutiny by the international community, there has begun to emerge a vocal but precarious civil societythat is, associations of individuals formed outside governmental structures to exchange ideas and information and to promote common interests and causes. Foremost among the interests bringing such associations into being has been the desire to promote respect for human rights. At first the government responded by detaining those who began openly to test the limits of official tolerance of human rights activity. This was then followed by a period of relative tolerance towards unofficial activities. A small number of Cubans took advantage of the apparently relaxed environment. These human rights activists produced press releases, met with foreigners and journalists, visited embassies and held meetings. What marks this period as one of relative tolerance is the fact that they were not imprisoned, though they continued to be harassed by the authorities. However, a recent string of arrests of members of an unofficial art group and others involved in human rights- related activities indicates that the tolerance may have been short-lived.

---

1   Similarly, Articles 287 to 294 of the penal code prohibit illegal house search, interference with correspondence, or with freedom of expression, association and religion. However, Americas Watch knows of no prosecutions or convictions on these grounds to date.

Dissenting voices have long been silenced by the Castro government in a variety of ways and with varying degrees of severity. Since the beginning of the revolution, the government has generally opted to imprison its opponents. Though exact numbers are not known, it is believed that at one time, there were as many as fifteen thousand, or perhaps twenty thousand, political prisoners in Cuban prisons. During Castro's first decade in power, several thousand prisoners were executed.[2] Castro, thereby, suppressed virtually all real or perceived opposition to his government. During the early 1980s, an unstable period marked by the "Mariel boatlift," it was not unusual for a peaceful critic of the government to be sentenced to up to 8 years in prison. More recently, critics and opponents of the government, branded "counterrevolutionaries" by government supporters, have been subjected to seemingly more lenient or more subtle forms of punishment. Dissenters have lost their jobs, have been harassed, sentenced to shorter prison terms, or imprisoned on technically non-political charges.

Several articles of the criminal code have been applied to those whose opinions do not conform with "the objectives of socialist society." "Enemy propaganda," considered a "crime against State security" a crime with acknowledged political overtonesis believed to be the most common charge brought against peaceful dissenters in the 1980s. During the earlier part of the decade, prison sentences were often for six or eight years, at the high end of the permissible range. Over the last two years, however, one of the steps the Cuban government seems to be taking to improve its image with respect to political imprisonment has been to shorten sentences for enemy propaganda. In addition, charges involving such common crimes as "contempt," "resistance," "public

---

2   Thomas, Hugh, The Cuban Revolution, Harper Torchbooks, 1977. At p. 684, Thomas cites
     Fidel Castro's acknowledgment in 1965 that there were then twenty thousand political
     prisoners and also writes that "The total number of executions probably reached 2,000 by
     early 1961, perhaps 5,000 by 1970." See also Valls, Jorge, Twenty Years and Forty Days,
     Americas Watch, 1986, for a memoir that reports frequent executions during the 1960s.

disorder," or "clandestine printing" have recently been brought against critics of the government. In this way, authorities may hope to avoid the international embarrassment that derives from incarcerating Cubans for crimes clearly involving the exercise of freedom of speech, and at the same time to continue to stifle peaceful expression.

The current criminal code which was adopted in December 1987 and went into effect in April 1988, is a reformed version of the 1979 criminal code. A number of minor common crimes were removed from the books, or the sentences were reduced. Most crimes that have been recently charged in political cases remain unchanged, however. In some cases, the sentences were increased.

"Enemy Propaganda"

The charge of "enemy propaganda," Article 103 of the current penal code, may be brought against anyone who "incites against social order, international solidarity or the socialist State" by producing, distributing or possessing oral, written or other "propaganda." Those found guilty may be deprived of liberty for one to eight years; for "diffusing false news or malicious predictions that tend to cause alarm or discontent or public disorder," they may be imprisoned for one to four years; if the mass media are used to carry out these crimes, one may be sentenced to seven to fifteen years; and anyone who permits the use of the mass media for these purposes may be sentenced to one to four years in prison.

Formerly Article 108, the crime of enemy propaganda was not otherwise altered under the new penal code. Enemy propaganda crimes are tried in the chamber of "crimes against state security," and appear in the penal code in a section with this heading that includes, among others, the crimes of rebellion and sabotage. Those convicted of enemy propaganda are imprisoned and held with other prisoners convicted of politically motivated crimes.

The case of Ariel Hidalgo Guillén is an example of the Cuban government's attitude towards opinions that are contrary to the ideology of the revolution. Hidalgo, now 43, was a professor of Marxism at the Manolito Aguiar Workers' College when he was imprisoned. His articles had been published in

10

official journals, and a book he wrote in 1976, *Origins of the Worker Movement and Socialist Thought in Cuba,* was used as a university textbook until he fell into disfavor.

Hidalgo was arrested on charges of enemy propaganda on August 19, 1981. During a search of his home by state security police, he was found to be in possession of his own original manuscript, *Cuba, The Marxist State and the New Class: A Dialectical Materialist Study,* and four extra copies. Hidalgo spent the next seven years in prison for writing an unpublished book that analyzes the current Cuban situation using Marxist methodology. Hidalgo believes he came under suspicion because, in addition to expressing criticism in the classroom of the government's response to those who sought to leave Cuba through the port of Mariel in 1980 which led state security officials to examine his students' notebook she himself sought to leave Cuba after he lost his teaching position.

At his trial, which lasted about half an hour, Hidalgo's court-appointed attorney's defense was that Hidalgo was young and could change his views. In the transcript of his trial, he was called a "leftist revisionist," and his sentence specified that his books should be burned.[3] Hidalgo was sentenced to eight years in prison. His release a year prior to the completion of his sentence is attributable to international pressure. He is now residing in the U.S. (See also Chapter 7, "Prison Conditions.")

Another example of the application of the enemy propaganda law to punish free expression is the case of Rafael Emilio Saumell Muñoz, 37, a writer now living in the U.S. who served a five-year prison term from 1981 to 1986 for his unpublished writings. Saumell was a member of UNEAC (Unión de Escritores y Artistas de Cuba), the official writers' union, and a former TV program director at the Cuban Institute for Radio and Television.

---

3   According to Hidalgo, the sentence read,"... y en cuanto a sus obras, destruyanse mediante el fuego." He does not know if any of his writings were actually burned.

His court transcript sheds light on the substance of an enemy propaganda trial and on the nature of the crime. Saumell is described as an "ideological enemy of socialism and the revolutionary process... dedicated to writing materials with counter-revolutionary content, abusive and denigrating to the leaders of the State and the Cuban Communist Party, or inciting against the social order, international solidarity and the Socialist State, having in his possession many such materials that were seized from his home on October 13, 1981, such as *Historia de una Infamia* (History of an Infamy), *El Automóvil* (The Automobile), *Cirilo el Jefe* (Cirilo the Boss), *Emilio Parodia mal a Baudelaire* (Emilio Parodies Baudelaire Poorly), *Me voy de viaje* (I am Going on a Trip) and others..." These are the titles of his short stories in manuscript form that were found during a house search by state security police after a colleague informed authorities that some of his short stories referred to those seeking refuge in the Peruvian Embassy and the events that led to the "Mariel boatlift." According to Saumell, his intention was not to write stories that were subversive or that could be construed as politically suspect. On the contrary, he had intended eventually to submit them to the Editorial Union of the Ministry of Culture UNEAC's imprint for publication.

Other recent cases involving the crime of enemy propaganda include:

- José Luis Alvarado Delgado, 24, was arrested in May 1982 and sentenced to six years in prison for attempting to mail photographs to the U.S. Interests Section in Havana. Alvarado had been released conditionally only months before he was rearrested in August 1986 for visiting the Reuters bureau to report on prison conditions. He was released again in March 1988 and seeks to emigrate. He was last denied an exit visa in October 1988. Alvarado has been active in the human rights movement.

- Francisco Benítez Ferrer, 23, former Navy officer, was sentenced to five years in prison in 1987, reportedly for writing on walls the thoughts of José Martí. He was granted early release in September 1988, but was reimprisoned on charges of "contempt" (*desacato*) reportedly for his attempts to meet with the U.N. Commission on Human Rights delegation. He is believed to be held in Combinado del Este prison.

- Marcos Carrillo Santana was sentenced in 1987 to 2 years for enemy propaganda. He is believed to have been released.
- Juan Castillo Pérez, an electrical engineer, was sentenced in 1983 to 12 years. He was also charged with "desertion" and "disobedience to orders," in connection with his refusal to serve in Angola. He is believed to be held in Combinado del Este prison.
- Eugenio Garay Sendin was sentenced in 1987 to 1 year and 4 months for his anti-government writings. He is believed to have been recently released.
- Fidel Silverio Vento Díaz was sentenced in 1986 to 1 1/2 years for enemy propaganda. He is believed to have been released upon completion of his term.

The following are prisoners believed to have been convicted of enemy propaganda for making anti-government posters. They are still held in or were recently released from Combinado del Este prison:

- Segundo González Alonso was reporteldy arrested in 1980 at the age of 16 and sentenced to 5 years in prison. He was held past completion of his sentence at least until early 1988. It is unclear whether or not he remains in prison.
- Pablo Andrés Betancourt Ramos was arrested in 1980 and sentenced to 10 years. He was released early in 1988.
- Raul Díaz Tejeda was arrested in 1987 and sentenced to 12 years. He was released in July 1988.
- Roberto Gil Mieres was sentenced in 1987 to 2 years. He was released in July 1988.
- Ramon Enrique Hernández Paez was sentenced in 1987 to 1 1/2 years. He is believed to be confined in Combinado del Este prison.
- Luis Antonio Núñez Acebo was sentenced in 1986 to 1 1/2 years, also for attempting to leave the country illegally and "escape." Nuñez was recently released from prison.
- Obel Piloto Montano was sentenced in 1987 to 1 year. He was released upon completion of his sentence.

- Julio A. Piquero Delgado was sentenced in 1987 to 1 year. He is believed to have been released upon completion of his sentence.
- Juan Lorenzo Ramírez Hernández was sentenced in 1987 to 2 years. He is believed to have been released.
- José Alberto Valdez Conde was sentenced in 1987 to 1 year. He has been released.
- Luis B. Quintero Perez, who had previously served a 4-year sentence for a book he wrote, was reimprisoned after another copy of the book was found. He is believed to be held in Combinado del Este prison. [dates not known]

"Contempt"

Article 144 of the current penal code, *desacato*, or contempt (or disrespect), has also been applied by the courts to punish critical speech or writing. Anyone who "threatens, slanders, defames, insults, injures, in any way outrages or offends, orally or in writing, the dignity or honor of an authority" may be imprisoned from three months to one year (up from three to nine months under the previous penal code). If the offense is committed against the President of the Council of State Fidel Castro or other heads and members of the highest State organs, it is punishable by one to three years in prison (up from six months to three years under the previous penal code). Contempt is considered a common crime. Those convicted of contempt serve their sentences along with common prisoners.

The case of Fernando Villalón Moreira exemplifies the use of this charge by Cuban authorities to punish critical speech. Villalón, now 27, was arrested on October 19, 1986 on charges of contempt for referring to Fidel Castro as a dictator and for refusing to vote in local elections in Santiago de Cuba. He is presently in Boniato prison in Santiago de Cuba where he is serving a three-year sentence along with common prisoners. Villalón is a former political prisoner who had been convicted of enemy propaganda in 1980 and sentenced to three years for putting up posters that were offensive to the government. (See also Appendix B, "Cases of Special Concern")

14

Rolando Ignacio Cartaya García, 35, a former music critic for the daily newspaper *Juventud Rebelde* who now lives in the U.S., served two years in prison for contempt. Cartaya was arrested in 1981 for writing an article which he intended to send to the Havana bureau of the Spanish press agency, EFE. The article criticized the Cuban government's handling of the Peruvian Embassy incident and the Mariel boatlift (See Chapter 3, "Freedom of Movement"). According to Cartaya, his degree from the Havana University School of Journalism was nullified, and he was unable to work as a journalist subsequent to his release.

Cartaya, who received a C-8 form from the Ministry of Interior in April 1986 which prevented him from leaving the country, was permitted to emigrate to the United States in May 1988. Cartaya has been a member of the Cuban Committee for Human Rights for several years.

"Public Disorder"

Desórdenes públicos, or public disorder, is punishable under Articles 200 and 201 of the current criminal code. Article 200 states that anyone who deliberately provokes panic or commotion in a public place or at a mass gathering by shouting false alarms may be sentenced to three months to one year in prison; if arms or explosives are used, one to three years in prison. Article 201 states that anyone who provokes quarrels or altercations in a public place, on public transport, or at public or social gatherings may be sentenced to three months to one year in prison. These provisions are not objectionable on their face. There is cause for concern, however, when they are invoked to suppress peaceful independent or unofficial associations.

In October 1988, Cuban authorities arrested six members of the *Asociación Pro Arte Libre* (the Association for Free Art, or APAL) (See also

Chapter 2, "Freedom of Association and Asssembly") a recently formed group advocating free expression and freedom of artistic creation. On October 20, the official *Día de la Cultura Cubana* (Cuban Culture Day), a group of about ten or twelve APAL members had gathered to place a floral wreath at a monument to José Martí[4] in Havana and to read a statement. According to a witness, a large group of people dressed in civilian clothes, believed to be state security police or encouraged by them, approached the group and began to assault the APAL members verbally and physically. Uniformed police arrived and arrested six APAL members, but none of their assailants. The APAL members were charged with public disorder and sentenced to terms ranging from seven months house arrest to one year in prison.

In November 1988, the President of the Cuban Human Rights Party was imprisoned along with two family members on charges of public disorder (see Chapter 2, "Freedom of Association and Assembly").

"Clandestine Printing"

While *clandestinidad de impresos*, or "clandestine printing" is ostensibly meant to discourage violation of what would be the equivalent of copyright laws in the U.S., this law has been invoked to punish those who attempt to produce writings that would not be published by government-owned presses, or that would be too dangerous to submit to a government-run publishing house. The charge of clandestine printing has been used particularly to curb the activities of Jehovah's Witnesses.

Article 241 of the 1979 penal code states:"[He] who produces, disseminates or directs the circulation of publications without indicating the press or the place of printing, or without complying with the rules established to identify an author or source, or reproduces, stores or transports them" may be im-

---

4   José Martí (1853-95) is embraced by both supporters and critics of the government as the Cuban national hero.

prisoned for three to nine months. In the 1987 penal code, Article 210 raises the maximum sentence to one year. Because the Constitution provides that all media are state property, all legal printed matter is published with offical consent by state-authorized authors and printing presses. If no printer or author is identified on a printed document, then it cannot be a state-authorized document and is illegal.

Several members of a Jehovah's Witness family have been repeatedly harassed by authorities, arrested and have served prison sentences in connection with their religious practices. At the end of January 1988, Joaquin Barthelemy Jiménez, 36, wasphysically assaulted and ordered to report to a police station by a state security agent who frequently checked up on the family. Barthelemy went to the police station the next day a half-hour early and left when he saw no one was there. He was violently apprehended and arrested on February 6 by the state security agent and charged with "clandestine printing," "escape" and "contempt." Barthelemy was acquitted of the last two charges and sentenced to seven months in prison for clandestineprinting. Fifteen minutes after he was detained, his home was searched by five state security agents and the President of the Committee for the Defense of the Revolution on his block (see Chapter 4, "Privacy and Surveillance"). The two books and three typed pages that were confiscated from his home were used as evidence against him at the trial. One book, *Happiness: How to Find it in Family Life*, appeared to be legal; the other, *From Paradise Lost to the Recovered Paradise*, was printed in 1957 (two years before the revolution) and may have been considered suspect for that reason. The three typed pages were copies of religious texts.

One of Joaquin's brothers was imprisoned for nine months on charges of "clandestine printing" between 1981 and 1982; and three months on charges of "illicit meeting"Article 240 of the 1979 penal codefor meeting with four co-religionists. Another brother was imprisoned for six months in connection with conversations and two papers in his possession related to his Jehovah's Witness practices.

Another case that has come to our attention is that of Israel Cabrera Bulgar who is believed to have been released from Boniato prison in March 1988 after serving six months for "clandestine printing." Cabrera, a Jehovah's

Witness, was found to be in possession of religious books and hymns and was accused of proselytism.

Media

As mentioned above, Article 52 establishes that all Cuban media are state property. According to the World Press Encyclopedia:

> In the early 1960s the Cubans introduced a Marxist media system, in which criticism of revolutionary goals was increasingly repressed, and Castro laid down the dictum that was to govern the role of the mass media in the new Cuban society:" For those within the Revolution, complete freedom; for those against the Revolution, no freedom."[5]

Today most Cuban publications are propaganda organs of government ministries, institutes, unions, associations and the Communist Party. The content of media coverage is predominantly positive news. Most Cuban editors and journalists are government-supporters or practice self-censorship. In order to practice the profession, journalists must belong to the Union of Cuban Journalists (UPEC) or the Cuban Institute of Radio and Television (ICRT). The Department of Revolutionary Orientation (DOR), coordinates "ideological policy among the editors, publishers, television and radio station managers as promulgated by the central committee of the party."[6] The Cuban press includes

---

5   Kurian, George Thomas edt., World Press Encyclopedia, Facts on File, Inc., 1982. The chapter on the Republic of Cuba is by John Spicer Nichols.

6   Harbron, John D., "Journalism in Cuba," Research Institute for Cuban Studies, Graduate School of International Studies, University of Miami, 1987.

over one hundred newspapers, magazines and journals; three national radio stations plus 120 medium-wave stations; and two television stations. Prensa Latina, Cuba's news agency, has 40 overseas bureaus.[7]

High-ranking government officials have acknowledged that the lack of tough or critical reporting has resulted in "boring" journalism. In 1980, Raul Castro used this adjective to describe the Cuban media in a speech to the Union of Cuban Journalists, asserting "criticism within our ranks is a political duty and social responsibility"; he added, "Criticize all you want! The Party is behind you!"[8] Seven years later, Fidel Castro stated in an interview with a French newspaper, "the press has to be much more critical and has to delve deeply into an analysis of problems."[9] In fact, the number of articles criticizing various particular or discrete aspects of Cuban society has increased in the last two years. However, journalists remain reluctant to pass judgment on essential principles of the system of government, on Cuba's top officials or on Cuba's military campaigns abroad. While the Soviet press has become bolder under Mikhail Gorbachev's policies of glasnost and perestroika, its Cuban counterpart, with

---

7   Ibid.

8   Kurian, Op. cit.

9   Martin, Lionel, "News Media in Cuba Show More Critical Candor," Reuters, October 17, 1988.

19

few exceptions, remains stifled under Fidel Castro's program of "rectification."[10]

Ironically, the Cuban media find it difficult even to report news from the Soviet Union. According to a Reuters story, "Reporting on the lively special [Communist Party] conference in Moscow, Cuba's state-controlled media seldom went beyond stating the obvious that it was about reform of the Soviet political and economic system... A Cuban journalist gasped when shown a news agency dispatch describing events at the conference."[11] Soviet media accessible to the Cuban public have proven to be very much in demand. A film from the Soviet Union, "Is It Easy To Be Young?" generally about discontent among Soviet youth, was due to be screened in Havana in the fall of 1987. It was withdrawn at the last minute, however, nearly causing a riot in front of the theater. The Spanish-language edition of Moscow News has become one of the most sought-after publications available in Cuba, an Americas Watch researcher was told by several persons during a visit to Cuba in early 1988.[12]

Several Cuban periodicals have boldly contributed to a debate about the emergence of an "information opening" (*apertura informativa*) in Cuba. In October 1987, the teen magazine *Somos Jovenes* ran a story entitled "The Case of Sandra" about prostitution, the drug trade and the black market phenomena

---

10 "Rectification" is nominally Cuba's counterpart to perestroika. Actually, it is the opposite of the Soviet Union's liberalizing trend. Since 1986, the rectification campaign has sought to correct the errors of the the revolution, such as corruption and inefficiency, through increasing government control of the economy and urging that Cubans work harder based on moral incentives.

11 Reuters, "Cuba public in the dark on glasnost," The Miami Herald, July 2, 1988.

12 See also Black, George, "Toward Victory Always, But When?" The Nation, October 24, 1988.

20

that had been officially wiped out by the revolution. However, the *Somos Jovenes* issue was immediately removed from the newsstands only to reappear without the prostitution article.[13]

The next month, *El Caiman Barbudo*, a literary magazine, published an article by a journalism student who criticized the Cuban press. The President of the Union of Cuban Journalists responded by asserting that the Cuban media should be "more revolutionary, more militant, and more communist." Though he conceded that the article made some valid points, he warned against a critical press that "invariably brings out extremist and liberal currents...opportunists and resentful people. These tendencies cannot wait... If some appealing formula appears on the international scene, [they] imitate it, immediately."[14]

Other Cuban publications that have carried unusually provocative stories in the last year include *Juventud Rebelde*, the newspaper of the Union of Communist Youth; and *Verde Olivo*, the magazine of the armed forces. Those journalists now testing the limits of government tolerance of a critical press would have done so at the risk of imprisonment in the past. Hubert Jerez, a former writer for Verde Olivo was detained and interrogated in Villa Marista for several weeks in 1985, after an article he wrote was found to be "problematical." He was later fired from the magazine. Another former journalist, Yndamiro Restano, who worked for Radio Rebelde, was detained briefly, demoted in his job and then fired after speaking with a U.S. newspaper correspondent

---

13   Ibid.

14   Ibid.

in 1985. Restano had also produced several isues of an independent newsletter on civil rights-related issues. Americas Watch has received several similar reports of journalists who were imprisoned on charges of "enemy propaganda" during the early 1980s, or simply fired from their jobs or expelled from the journalists or writers union. It is encouraging to note that the response of government officials to critical journalists or journalism students recently has been debate rather than punishment.

Numerous western press agencies maintain bureaus in Havana. Representatives of the U.S. press are not permitted to maintain offices in Cuba,[15] although U.S. correspondents are allowed to travel to Cuba several times a year, especially during national celebrations and festivals. Foreign correspondents are generally tolerated. Harassment of foreign journalists is not unknown in Cuba, however.

In June 1985, the Agence France-Presse (AFP) bureau chief was expelled from Cuba for writing an article that "denigrated" Cuban women and was considered "an outrage to national dignity." The article claimed that foreigners who wished to marry Cuban women were required to pay a "bride price" in administrative fees to a semi-official agency.[16]

---

15   Prensa Latina is accredited and has a bureau at the United Nations in New York. However, Cuban journalists are not permitted to be based in the U.S. The Prensa Latina correspondents at the U.N. are subject to travel restrictions -- they may not travel more than 25 miles from the U.N.. Other journalists from Cuba are occasionally permitted to travel to the U.S. to cover special events. For instance, Cuban journalists travelled to New York with the Cuban delegation for the tri-partite talks among Cuba, Angola and South Africa. Prensa Latina correspondents have also been permitted to travel to Washington, D.C. from Cuba.

16   Committee to Protect Journalists, CPJ Update, July/August 1985.

Foreign correspondents have been harassed by Cuban authorities particularly for contact with the human rights community. In September 1983, two French journalists were detained by state security police for ten days and then expelled from Cuba after meeting with human rights activist Ricardo Bofill. In September 1986, the Reuters bureau chief and an AFP correspondent were expelled after speaking with human rights activist Elizardo Sánchez.

In July 1988, a *Washington Post* reporter included at the end of an article, "This reporter was followed for several hours through the streets of Havana by a state-owned vehicle after leaving [Ricardo] Bofill's home."[17] In January 1989, the same reporter wrote, "Two journalists who visited [Elizardo Sanchez] last weekend were reprimanded within a matter of hours by Foreign Ministry officials."[18]

In December 1988, a Canadian Broadcasting Corporation (CBC) radio correspondent was strongly advised by an officer of the Cuban Institute for Radio and Television not to seek out interviews with Cubans who can report human rights violations, such as those who are not permitted to leave the country and human rights activists. That correspondent also reported that two journalists -- for Radio Canada -- were called into the Cuban Foreign Ministry and berated for meeting with members of Cuba's human rights community.

The mainstream U.S. press is not generally available to the Cuban public. Radio Martí, a program of the U.S. Information Agency, is broadcast

---

17   Preston, Julia, "Cuban Dissident Tries to Form Party," The Washington Post, July 28, 1988.

18   Preston, Julia, "Cuba Says It Will Free Last Political Prisoners," The Washington Post, January 4, 1989.

to Cuba against Fidel Castro's objections. Aside from this source, news from U.S. sources can be obtained only through contacts with foreigners. In December 1988, the Cuban government warned the U.S. Interests Section that it was not permitted to distribute American publications without authorization. The protest was in response to the Interests Section's practice of distributing extra copies of magazines and newspapers it receives to a limited number of people. Cuban authorities were reportedly most annoyed by the circulation of newspapers published in Miami.[19]

The existing legal guarantees affecting the fundamental human right of freedom of expression do more to hinder than to protect it. Cuba has none of the mechanisms that could help to ensure freedom of expression for its citizens such as an independent judiciary, legislature, opposition political parties, or press and labor unions that are independent of the government. Until the Cuban government permits the establishment of such institutions and associations, and abolishes the restrictions that permeate its laws, freedom of expression remains a matter of executive grace in Cuba. At that, the Cuban government has shown little indication that it will manifest such grace.

---

19   Ojito, Mirta, "Castro Prohibe Publicaciones de EU," El Nuevo Herald, December 23, 1988. It is worth mentioning that access to information from Cuba in the U.S. until recently has been limited almost exclusively to academic institutions and libraries. In August 1988, the Reagan Administration endorsed a trade bill that lifts restrictions on the importation of Cuban books, films and records. In theory, these items may now become commercially available to a wider audience in the U.S.

FREEDOM OF ASSOCIATION AND ASSEMBLY

All Cubans have the right to participate in a variety of social, political, labor, cultural, and other "mass organizations" under the control of the government. Through participation in these officially-imposed structures, Cubans may demonstrate their level of "integration" in the society that is, their level of support for the government. It is virtually impossible to participate in similar activities independent of those organizations prescribed by the government. To attempt to do so clandestinely will invariably be noticed by Cuba's neighborhood surveillance committees, the CDRs (see Chapter 4, "Privacy and Surveillance") and may be construed as activity that is hostile towards the government. Those who have openly exercised freedom of association and assembly have done so at the risk of persecution and imprisonment.

Nevertheless, during the recent period of greater access to Cuba by international human rights organizations, a number of Cubans have taken advantage of the protection afforded by these visits to test the limits of the Castro government's tolerance of an independent and peaceful civil society. Groups that had until recently operated "underground," cautiously and discreetly, have openly held unofficial gatherings and have increased their contact with the press and with the diplomatic and international human rights communities. In addition, in 1988 a number of new groups formed and assumed a public posture from the outset. Though the emergence of these groups has given the appearance of greater openness and of an improved human rights environment in Cuba, incidents of continuing repression indicate that freedom of association and assembly remain tenuous undertakings subject to arbitrary reprisals.

Article 20 of the Universal Declaration of Human Rights provides that "Everyone has the right to freedom of peaceful assembly and association," and "No one may be compelled to belong to an association."

The Cuban Constitution grants these rights in a restricted form, effectively divesting them of meaning. Article 53 of the Constitution states:

> The rights of assembly, demonstration and association are exercised by workers, both manual and intellectual, peasants, women, students and other sectors of the working people, for which they are provided with the necessary means.
>
> The social and mass organizations have all the facilities they need to carry out those activities in which the members have full freedom of speech and opinion based on the unlimited right of initiative and criticism.

When examined in light of Article 61 which specifies that the freedoms guaranteed to Cuban citizens may not be "exercised against... the existence and objectives of socialist State," however, it becomes clear that the constitutional provision regarding association is meaningful only to government-supporters. Indeed, in light of the prohibitions on "illicit associations, gatherings and demonstrations" in Articles 208 and 209 of the current penal code, Cuban law provides no protection for the exercise of the internationally recognized right of freedom of peaceful assembly and association. Under Articles 208 and 209, for belonging to an unregistered association, or participating in unauthorized gatherings or demonstrations, one could serve one to three months in prison; for leading an unregistered association, or organizing unauthorized gatherings or demonstrations, three months to one year (up from the previous maximum of nine months).

Human Rights Groups

The most outspoken of the independent groups that have emerged in Cuba are human rights groups: the Cuban Committee for Human Rights (*Comité Cubano Pro-Derechos Humanos* -- CCPDH) and the Cuban Commission for Human Rights and National Reconciliation (*Comisión Cubana de Derechos Humanos y Reconciliación Nacional* -- CCDHRN). Both CCPDH and CCDHRN have petitioned the Ministry of Justice for legal registration, but to date have received no response.

Though the two groups (which started out as a single group) have endured setbacks during the last two years, they have made significant progress in creating a tiny space for criticism of human rights conditions in Cuba. They have been best able to function, and their activities most tolerated, when international attention is focused on Cuba, whether through visits by foreigners or debates within the U.N. To appreciate the changes that have taken place in the human rights climate as it exists today, it can be compared with the last major crackdown on human rights monitors in 1986.

José Luis Alvarado, a member of CCPDH, was arrested in late August 1986 after giving statements on prison conditions to the Reuters news agency in Havana. Three months earlier Alvarado had been conditionally released from serving a six-year prison term on charges of enemy propaganda. (See Chapter 1, "Freedom of Expression") Around the same time, a report of a death in state security detention was circulating in the human rights community.[1] On August 27, Ricardo Bofill, President of CCPDH, sought refuge in the French Embassy in Havana. Bofill did not emerge from his refuge in the French Embassy for five months, at the end of January 1987.[2]

In September 1986, after speaking with foreign correspondents in Havana, Elizardo Sánchez, then Vice President of CCPDH, was detained along with Enrique Hernández Méndez, Adolfo Rivero Caro and Samuel Martínez Lara, members of CCPDH. They were held in state security detention without

---

[1]   Americas Watch has been unable to confirm information on the death in state security detention of Antonio Frias Sosa in August 1986. According to Cuban authorities, Frias committed suicide by jumping out a window. His family was immediately notified and his body was returned to them. It is unclear whether Frias was a member of CCPDH or to what extent he was involved in human rights activities.

[2]   According to an official of the French government with whom Americas Watch spoke while Bofill was in the Embassy, Cuban authorities had threatened to enter the Embassy to arrest him. The French authorities made clear that this could cause a disruption in relations, and no effort was made to arrest Bofill. Indeed, even when he left the Embassy in January 1987, he was permitted to return to his home without interference.

charge for varying lengths of time. A few days after they were detained, the Havana-based correspondents from Agence France-Presse and Reuters with whom Sánchez spoke were expelled from Cuba. Hernández, Rivero and Martínez were released from detention five months later in February 1987, on the eve of the start of the U.N. Commission on Human Rights session in Geneva. Sánchez was released eight months later, the following May.

During this period, in Combinado del Este prison, a political prisoner who was an active member of CCPDH, Ariel Hidalgo, went on hunger strike to protest the persecution of his fellow human rights activists outside. In retaliation, according to Hidalgo, he was moved to a punishment cell in the "rectangle of death" where he was held for 5 1/2 days without drinking water, his only sustenance.

After this period of persecution, these human rights activists enjoyed a relatively relaxed climate between mid-1987 and early 1988. They met with the foreign press, including visiting correspondents from *The New York Times*, *The Miami Herald* and *The Los Angeles Times*, with members of Americas Watch, as well as with other visiting foreigners. Differences between Bofill and Sánchez led them to separate into two groups and in October 1987, Sánchez formed CCDHRN. Nevertheless, both Ricardo Bofill and Elizardo Sánchez each continued to hold press conferences to which journalists and diplomats were invited to listen to the testimony of ex-political prisoners, family members of current political prisoners, failed political asylum-seekers and other members of Cuba's persecuted. Members of both groups maintained contact with the U.S. Interests Section in Havana. Bofill, along with several dozen CCPDH sympathizers attended services in a Havana church every Sunday using the occasions to assemble with each other while avoiding actual activity that might be labelled as "illicit." With his sight set on the U.N. Human Rights Commission in Geneva, Bofill released a human rights report for 1987 to journalists, diplomats and international human rights organizations at the end of that year.

By then the human rights activists were beginning once again to reach the limits of government tolerance. On January 26, 1988, Bofill and two other members of CCPDH, Rolando Cartaya and Rafael Saumell Muñoz, were detained by state security police. They were held several hours for questioning on the eve of a human rights press conference they planned, to which representatives of various embassies and the press had been invited. The fact that none of the human rights activists was charged and imprisoned was an encouraging sign, however.

On February 13, CCPDH held what is believed to have been the first independent art exhibit in Cuba since the revolution. It was held in the home of CCPDH members and featured the "afro-cuban" works of an artist who, inspired by the history of slavery in Cuba in the 19th century, explores the legacy of that history. Also on display were works of art and written works by former and current political prisoners. Bofill and other members of the CCPDH took the opportunity to report on violations of human rights in Cuba.

A number of foreign correspondents and diplomats were present, as well as a visiting delegation of the Association of the Bar of the City of New York that included members of Americas Watch. Though the exhibit was held without incident, Bofill announced that several members of the press and diplomatic corps had been telephoned by unknown callers that morning and informed that the exhibit was cancelled. Nevertheless, the exhibit had a remarkable turnout, though mostly foreigners.

The government's attitude became increasingly hostile towards this activity, however, when four days later, CCPDH opened the exhibit again so that those who had stayed away on the 13th would have another chance to see the exhibit and listen to the group. This time, the gathering was reportedly interrupted by an aggressive crowd of neighbors that formed outside the house in what was supposed to appear to be a spontaneous display of disapproval. The angry mob verbally and physically assaulted those attending the exhibit and the

Cuban police arrived, ostensibly to protect them from the crowd. Subsequently, some of those present at the exhibit told a representative of Americas Watch that they had recognized some of those in the "mob" as the same individuals who at other times engaged in surveillance of them.

One month later, the human rights monitors, especially Bofill, were subjected to numerous virulent attacks in the Cuban media including long articles in the Communist Party daily *Granma*, the humor magazine Palante, and a three-part television series.[3] This attempt to discredit the human rights monitors came in the aftermath of the U.N. Commission on Human Rights meetings in Geneva in March 1988.

There followed a period of relative calm marked by a visit in April by John Cardinal O'Connor of New York during which he highlighted the plight of political prisoners, until finally agreeing with Fidel Castro on the release of several hundred political prisoners. Just three months later, however, on July 14, 1988, Jesus Leyva Guerra, a human rights activist who reported to both CCPDH and CCDHRN, was detained and confined in the *pabellón judicial* (judicial ward) of the psychiatric hospital in Santiago de Cuba where he remains today (see Chapter 7, "Prison Conditions," section on psychiatric confinement). Leyva, who had reported on the harassment of Pentecostals in Santiago de Cuba

---

3   Members of two delegations that had visited Cuba earlier in the year, from the Association of the Bar of the City of New York and the Institute for Policy Studies, were secretly filmed in the course of their contact with CCPDH and were shown on the program. A member of the Bar Association delegation was filmed in the street upon first meeting Bofill. The IPS group was filmed at the church that is attended by Bofill and some of those associated with him.

during the spring of 1988,[4] was reportedly detained by state security police while gathering testimony of human rights violations in a private home. This was the first long-term detention of a human rights activist since the release of Elizardo Sánchez in May 1987 that has come to the attention of Americas Watch.

Soon afterwards, in a revealing incident that reached international proportions, the Cuban Foreign Ministry made it known that it considered a gathering of U.S. diplomats and Cuban human rights monitors "an interference in the internal affairs of Cuba."[5] The Cuban government revoked the visas issued to Representative Dan Mica of Florida and five Congressional aides in reprisal for a cocktail party held at the home of U.S. Press Attache Jerry Scott on July 15. Twenty or thirty Cuban human rights activists, former political prisoners, artists and intellectuals had been invited to Scott's home. The Cuban Foreign Ministry statement referred to the human rights monitors as "counter-revolutionary ex-prisoners" and "antisocial elements," charging that U.S. officials were advising the Cubans with respect to the upcoming visit by the UNCHR "to promote a deformed image of Cuban reality."[6] The statement concluded: "The Ministry of Foreign Relations expects, that in the future, the officials of the U.S. Interests Section will abstain from carrying out activities of this nature and reiterates that they should reflect on the consequences of actions that are inadmissible and which will not be tolerated by our authorities."[7] The U.S. strongly protested the Cuban action. Representative Mica had sought to

---

4   Americas Watch received reports of harassment of Pentecostals and interference in their church services in Santiago de Cuba in the spring of 1988. A pastor of the church, Orson Vila Santoyo, was reportedly arrested and on May 19 was tried in the provincial court of Holguín on charges of holding "illicit gatherings" and "preaching against public health." Vila was sentenced to five months in prison. On appeal, his sentence was commuted to a fine.

5   FBIS-LAT, 22 July 1988.

6   Ibid.

7   Ibid.

go to Cuba to look into security problems at the U.S. Interests Section in Havana. He was permitted to conduct this investigation the next month.

Greater freedom of movement is one of the primary goals of human rights activists in Cuba. Compliance with this right by the Cuban government on any level is welcome. During 1988, a significant number of Cuban human rights activists, including Ricardo Bofill, leader of CCPDH, were permitted to emigrate, most after years of repeated denial. (See Chapter 3, "Freedom of Movement") Permission for a three-month visit to the U.S. by Elizardo Sánchez during the summer of 1988 was another positive step. By themselves, however, these measures by no means establish a pattern of freedom of movement that may be followed by other government critics. Rather, they seem to be arbitrary concessions to the international human rights community.

Other Associations

The period of tolerance, though it continues to be interrupted by occasional reprisals, has permitted the emergence of some other independent activities by a growing number of emboldened Cubans. Their experience also underscores the limited nature of government tolerance.

The existence of the "Eco-Pacifist Movement (*Movimiento Eco-Pacifista*), an anti-war and anti-nuclear group, was brought to our attention in 1988. Its President, Orlando Polo, has made numerous walks dating back to 1985, from nearly one end of the island to the other, sometimes with his wife, Mercedes Paez, stopping in public places to speak to assembled crowds. Polo, who has also been associated with both CCPDH and CCDHRN, advocates peace and protests Cuban involvement in Angola. He has been detained almost two dozen times during these walks. In addition, Polo and Paez are leaders of a vegetarian group, known as the "Life Naturist Association" (*Asociación Naturista Vida*), which is said to have been originally founded in 1935 by Spanish anarchists. The association, based on a farm outside Havana, boasts 150 members. In April 1988, the Supreme Court ordered the dissolution of the vegetarian society which could mean confiscation of the farm. To date, however, Cuban authorities have not interfered with Vida's activities.

32

In a similar vein, Julio Soto Angurel, who reportedly served in a civilian capacity for the Cuban armed forces in Angola, issues statements in support of *perestroika* and *glasnost* under the banner of the "José Martí Association of Independent Defenders of Human Rights and Reconciliation" (*Conjunto de Defensores Independientes de los Derechos Humanos y la Reconciliación Nacional, José Martí*). Soto was reportedly expelled from ICAIC, the national film institute, in the early 1970s, for a disparaging comment about prices in Cuba. When asked by a representative of Americas Watch about the difference between his organization and the CCPDH and the CCDHRN, Soto said that his organization was not made up of former prisoners. It is not known how many persons are associated with Soto's group.

An independent masonic organization *Estrella de Cuba*, was reportedly founded in August 1988 shortly after its founder was expelled from the officially-recognized masonic order for planning to hold a human rights conference. *Estrella de Cuba* is a clandestine association which attempts to promote activities similar to those of the Grand Lodge of Cuba in a freer atmosphere as well as respect for a diversity of ideological and political opinions.

The Martí Civic League (*Liga Cívica Martiana*) was formed in July 1986 by a group of twelve political prisoners in Combinado del Este prison whose goal was to inform Cubans "on the street" about human rights violations in their country. Attempting to go beyond simply reporting abuses to the international community, they aimed to raise consciousness in the population and urge Cubans to demand the government's respect for their rights. They also support amnesty for all political prisoners, an end to obligatory military service and military intervention abroad and the abolition of the death penalty. To carry out its mission, the Martí Civic League established an information network in which writings from prison would be circulated from person to person in a "reading circle," and then passed to another reading circle. Up to three hundred people are said to participate clandestinely in the league.

Aurora, the journal produced in prison by the founders of the Martí Civic League, has voiced the concerns of political prisoners since 1986. Several originals were produced of each issue, of which there are believed to be eleven to date. Some circulated in the prisons and some were smuggled out to be copied

33

and distributed. *Aurora* published essays, poetry and some illustrations related to human rights themes, such as the persecution of peaceful dissenters and conditions in prison. Other journals produced by political prisoners include *Disidente* and two recent publications, *Paz, Amor y Libertad*, and *El Martiano*.

JARPE (*Junta de Autodefensa de Religiosos Perseguidos*) was founded in Combinado del Este prison in 1985 to provide a support network for those who have been persecuted for their religious practices or those who simply wished to practice their religion in prison and were prevented from doing so by authorities. JARPE is a multi-denominational Christian association reportedly with up to 120 members in prison. Since pastoral visits have not been permitted in Cuban prisons,[8] they hold their own services and distribute the sermons. They have also engaged in hunger strikes to obtain permission to receive religious materials.

Unofficial theater troupes, performance artists and groups of intellectuals have been reported as being both vocal and visible in their criticism of the government.[9] Americas Watch is heartened by the peaceful activities of these groups and others that perhaps remain unknown to us. We urge the Cuban government to tolerate the civil society that is striving to emerge.

---

[8] It was recently reported that the Cuban Catholic Church is negotiating an agreement with the government to allow pastoral visits in the prisons. Sawyer, Jon, "Apertura: Cuba's Sporadic Glasnost," St. Louis Post-Dispatch, November 21, 1988. When an Americas Watch representative raised the question of pastoral visits with the Minister of Justice of Cuba in March 1988, he denied knowing of any interest in such visits by the Church.

[9] Ibid.

New Crackdown

Regrettably, the Cuban government has once again begun to crack down on its critics. In the fall of 1988, Cuban authorities detained an undetermined number of its citizens in connection with human rights activity. Though Americas Watch notes that some detentions were brief and some prison terms were short in comparison to previous years, we abhor the continuing punishment of peaceful dissent in Cuba.

The delegation of the U.N. Commission on Human Rights, which conducted a human rights investigation in Cuba from September 16 to 25, 1988, arranged for Cubans who sought to raise their cases or report human rights abuses to go to the Hotel Comodoro in Havana. During the week of September 19, two incidents in front of the hotel led to the arrest of an unknown number of persons. Reportedly, on September 19, when the UN delegation returned from an appointment outside the hotel, the crowd waiting to see them broke into applause and cheers. After the delegation entered the hotel, the police arrested a number of people, took them to the Villa Marista state security facility, fined them, and eventually released them. Then on September 21, the police stationed in front of the hotel had been harassing some of those waiting to meet with the delegation and reportedly prevented or threatened to prevent some of those individuals from entering the hotel. An undetermined number of people are believed to have been arrested as a result. Some of those detained that week were held for several hours, others for several days. Still others were reportedly arrested or rearrested and held for varying lengths of time after the U.N. Commission delegation left Cuba. At this writing, it remains unclear exactly when and under what circumstances many of them were arrested (see Appendix A, "The Persecution of Human Rights Monitors").

Among those arrested on September 21 was a former political prisoner, Gustavo Venta Pérez, who staged a fast in front of the hotel to urge the release of all political prisoners and in support of the work of the U.N. Commission and domestic human rights groups in Cuba. Reportedly, Venta was first taken to a police station and from there transferred to the state security facility, Villa Marista, where he was seriously mistreated and beaten. He was tried in the Municipal Court of Playa and sentenced to six months in prison on charges of contempt (*desacato*) and resistance. He has reportedly attempted to appeal his sentence three times and each time the hearing was suspended because witnesses for the prosecution -- in this case state security police -- have failed to appear in court. Venta is serving his sentence in Combinado del Este prison.

Francisco Benítez Ferrer, a recently released political prisoner, and his brother, Alejandro, also are believed to have been arrested in connection with their attempt to see the U.N. Commission delegation. They were tried and sentenced on charges of contempt and/or resistance to six months and three months in prison, respectively. Francisco Benítez is serving his term in Combinado del Este prison. It is unclear where Alejandro is being held.

Elizardo Sánchez was openly followed by state security agents in September upon his return from a three-month visit to the U.S. and during the visit of the U.N. Commission, with which his group met. Several weeks later, after being subjected to increasing pressures at work, Sánchez was fired from his job at a library in Havana.

Pablo Llabre Raurell, a member of CCPDH, was reportedly subjected to a so-called *acto de repudio*, or "act of repudiation" on September 28, the twenty-eighth anniversary of the Committees for the Defense of the Revolution (See Chapter 4, "Privacy and Surveillance"). Members of the local CDRs gathered in front of his home in Havana and, using loudspeakers, verbally assaulted Llabre and denounced his participation in human rights activities.

The Association for Free Art (*Asociación Pro Arte Libre*, APAL; see also Chapter 1, "Freedom of Expression"), a group advocating free expression and freedom of artistic creation, is believed to have formed in August 1988. Several members of APAL have been members of the Cuban Committee for Human Rights and have begun to initiate similar activities. Its leaders reportedly also have submitted a petition to the Ministry of Justice requesting official registration. To date, however, they have received no response and remain an unofficial group. The Association for Free Art is said to be divided into two sections. APAL members have participated in meetings with other independent groups in Cuba and are believed to have met with or attempted to meet with the

U.N. human rights delegation. Tolerance of this new group, however, was short-lived.

During the last two weeks of October, six people believed to be affiliated with one APAL section were detained under unknown circumstances and taken to the Havana state security facility, Villa Marista. Five of the six -- Pablo Roberto Pupo Sánchez, Juan Enrique García, Lázaro Cabrera Puentes,[10] Ramón Obregón Sarduy and Gilberto Plasencia Jiménez -- are in their third month of detention without trial. The sixth, León Alex Matos Cabrera, was reportedly released in mid-November. Although they reportedly have not been seriously mistreated and have been permitted visits by family members, none have had access to counsel.

On October 20, six members of the other APAL section were arrested at the site of their peaceful commemoration of Cuban Culture Day (See Chapter 1, "Freedom of Expression"). They were tried four days later and convicted on charges of "public disorder." Their sentences were later upheld on appeal. Armando Araya García is serving one year in prison; Octavio Vladimir García Alderete and Rita Fleitas Fernández are serving nine months in prison; Secundino Hernández Castro and David Ornedo García are serving seven months in prison; and Aída Valdez Santana is serving seven months under house arrest for reasons of health. Americas Watch is disturbed by reports that Octavio Vladimir García Alderete has been on hunger strike for several weeks in Combinado del Este prison to claim his political status.

Havana Tele-Rebelde and Havana Radio Rebelde networks provided the following accounts of the incident:

> The National Revolutionary Police reported that around
> 19:30 yesterday evening approximately one dozen persons
> hostile to the revolution began provocative activities at the

---

10   Lazaro Cabrera Puentes may have been detained in connection with his reported attempt
      to seek refuge or asylum in the Embassy of the Federal Republic of Germany.

37

park located on Carcel Street between Prado and Martires Avenue, next to the monument of the national hero.

Immediately and spontaneously, persons in the area gave a revolutionary and strong response by holding a meeting to express their repudiation of and combativeness toward such acts.

As a result of the incident, the police arrested six antisocial persons who will be tried by the courts. [FBIS-LAT, 24 October 1988.]; and

On October 20, close to a dozen people opposed to the revolution congregated... and tried to conduct a provocative activity that was thwarted by people from the area, the majority of whom were youths who learned that the acts were of a counterrevolutionary nature.

The incident justly caused the people to repel the act and this was immediately and strongly expressed.[11]

In early July 1988, the Cuban Human Rights Party (*Partido Cubano Pro Derechos Humanos*) was formed by members of CCPDH. Its main objective has been to collect signatures on petitions in support of changes in Cuban law to be submitted to the National Assembly of People's Power, the legislative organ of

---

11   FBIS-LAT, 26 October 1988.

the government. A few weeks later, Fidel Castro expressed his strong disapproval of a second political party in Cuba. In his annual 26 of July[12] speech, Castro asserted that there was no need for more than one party "in the same way that Lenin didn't need more than one party to make the October Revolution... no one should have any illusions that we are going to begin to allow pocket parties in Cuba, to organize the counterrevolutionaries, the bourgeois and the Yankee-lover."[13]

No reprisals were taken against the Cuban Human Rights Party until November, when the President of the party, Tania Díaz Castro, a published poet and former journalist for Bohemia, was arrested with her son and daughter-in-law and summarily tried and imprisoned, all in the same day. On November 29, Diaz and her father, along with Guillermo Rivas Díaz and Aimee Llado Cantón, her son and daughter-in-law, went to Combinado del Este prison to visit several prisoners including Rivas Díaz's father. Guillermo Rivas Díaz is the son of Guillermo Rivas Porta, a long-term prisoner, *plantado*, who at the time was serving over 21 years in prison. When Díaz's father and daughter-in-law were arbitrarily prohibited from entering the prison, they protested and then a fist fight ensued between them and the prison guards. They were then arrested -- with the exception of Díaz's 74-year old grandfather -- and taken to a police station near the prison.

---

12   July 26, 1953, the day of the assault on the Moncada barracks in Santiago de Cuba of Fulgencio Batista's armed forces, is celebrated as the beginning of Castro's revolutionary movement.

13   Preston, Julia, "Cuban Dissident Tries to Form Party," Washington Post, July 28, 1988. The government's attitude was similar in response to the one hundred writers, actors and other well-known personalities who signed a petition calling on Fidel Castro to hold a plebiscite on his government, among other things. The petition was published as an advertisement in The New York Times and other newspapers on December 27, 1988. According to Prensa Latina, the Cuban Foreign Ministry's answer included the statement,"The Cuban people held a grand plebiscite concerning their destiny 30 years ago and they repeat that action every day with their decision to continue with socialism." See Associated Press, "Cuba Says Petition for Vote On Castro's Rule is Absurd," The New York Times, December 29, 1988.

About two hours later, they were summarily tried and convicted on charges of public disorder (see Chapter 5, "Due Process"). Tania Díaz Castro and Aimee Llado Cantón were sentenced to one year and three months respectively in the women's prison outside Havana (*Centro de Reeducación de Mujeres de Occidente*). Guillermo Rivas Díaz was sentenced to one year in Combinado del Este prison. He and several *plantados*, including his father, went on hunger strike to protest the incident.

On January 3, 1988, Guillermo Rivas Porta, Guillermo Rivas Díaz and Aimee Llado Cantón were released from prison and flown directly to the U.S. Americas Watch welcomes their release. However, we remain concerned about the continuing imprisonment of Tania Díaz Castro.

Another member of the Cuban Human Rights Party, Hiram Abi Cobas Nuñez, was reportedly detained on January 12, 1988 on his way to work. He was held in a regular police station in Havana, *2da unidad de Centro Habana*, incommunicado for approximately thirty-six hours. He was reporteldy fined 300 pesos for "clandestine printing." Cobas is said to have been in possession of a copy of the Human Rights Party's newsletter, *Franqueza*. Although Americas Watch, under these circumstances, does not support any form of punishment for being in possession of a newsletter, we are encouraged that Mr. Cobas was fined rather than imprisoned.

Americas Watch has received reports of other incidents of harassment of human rights activists that occurred in recent months, such as physical assaults on the street by groups of unidentified persons.

It has become clear that tolerance of emerging human rights monitoring activity in Cuba is limited and subject to arbitrary lapses. As long as tolerance of the peaceful expression of opinions by such groups and individuals is not recognized in law, Cuban human rights monitors will remain vulnerable to persecution. The latitude afforded the two human rights groups would be more convincing and, indeed, commendable if the government would grant them official permission to function without fear, as by legal registration by the Ministry of Justice.

FREEDOM OF MOVEMENT

Cuban Law and International Standards

Over the last three years, more than 200 Cuban refugees landed along the coast of southern Florida on inner tubes, rafts and small boats, fleeing Cuba illegally. These crossings dramatize the severe restrictions that have been placed on emigration by the Cuban government.

Under the Universal Declaration of Human Rights, "everyone has the right to freedom of movement and residence within the borders of each State" and "to leave any country, including his own, and to return to his country" (Article 13). The Cuban Constitution does not guarantee its citizens the right to leave and return to Cuba, however. Indeed, the Cuban government regularly violates these internationally recognized human rights. Moreover, the Cuban government severely punishes those who break Cuban law by attempting to leave the country illegally, or to seek political asylum abroad or to seek refuge in foreign embassies in Havana.

In this context, "the right to seek and to enjoy in other countries asylum from persecution" -- Article 14 of the Universal Declaration of Human Rights -- takes on a complex meaning. Cuban citizens have attempted to leave the country by seeking refuge in foreign embassies in Havana rather than risk reprisal by formally applying to emigrate, and rather than risk imprisonment by attempting to leave the country clandestinely. Some Cubans have entered embassies employing force, and have been imprisoned for long periods as a result.

Under Article 216 of the current penal code it is illegal to leave or to prepare an attempt to leave the country "without complying with the legal formalities" -- *salida ilegal del territorio nacional.* This crime is punishable by one to three years imprisonment (formerly six months to three years under Article 247 of the 1979 penal code). The use of violence, intimidation or force while at-

41

tempting to leave the country is punishable by three to eight years imprisonment.

Organizing, promoting or inciting *salida ilegal* may lead to two to five years imprisonment, under Article 217 of the new penal code. This is a higher sentence than was provided in Article 248 of the previous penal code, which was one to four years. Lending material aid, offering information or in any way facilitating *salida ilegal* incurs a sentence of one to three years (previously six months to three years).

According to Amnesty International, the Cuban government claims that 574 people were arrested and imprisoned in 1987 for attempting to leave the country illegally; that is, without the permission of the Cuban government (see Chapter 6, "Detention Procedures"). Cuban authorities do not consider these persons to be political prisoners and, therefore, they are held with common prisoners.

"Acts that affect the right of extraterritoriality" is the penal code article that has been applied to those convicted of forcibly entering a foreign embassy. Article 249 of the 1979 penal code, under which the cases of concern to Americas Watch were prosecuted, established a prison sentence of one to eight years for this crime. Under Article 218 of the new penal code, which punishes "acts that affect the right of diplomatic inviolability," the minimum sentence is increased and the maximum reduced to two to five years in prison.

Restrictions on Freedom of Movement Across Cuban Borders

Because even applying for permission to emigrate is seen as a gesture of discontent with the revolution, many are inhibited by the prospect of extra-legal retaliation. Once you are perceived as "disaffected," it is no longer in the interest of your superior to keep you in your job; a colleague who is better "integrated" in the revolution, will probably be found to be better suited for a promotion; a student whose family plans to emigrate may not be considered as deserving of a place at the university as another who is an enthusiastic participant in the activities of the communist youth union; your acquaintances at work or school, or your neighbors may feel compelled to demonstrate their disapproval of your efforts to leave the country, once it becomes common knowledge; and so on. Those who plan to leave the country permanently must give up their home and property, except personal belongings.[1]

Guillermo Rivas Díaz, the son of human rights activist Tania Díaz Castro and Guillermo Rivas Porta, a *plantado* who was released in January 1989 after over 21 years in prison, was penalized for expressing the desire to leave Cuba. In June 1987, he was fired from his job at the telephone company after his superiors learned that he had decided to leave Cuba with his father upon his release from prison. The next month, Rivas Díaz's wife, Aimee Llado Cantón, was fired from her job at a bank.

Cubans seeking to emigrate were met with much more extreme forms of retaliation during the spring and summer of 1980, at the time of the "Mariel boatlift." Committees for the Defense of the Revolution (CDRs) were directed, and government supporters were encouraged by them, to engage aggressively in verbal abuse, stone-throwing, severe beatings, vandalism of homes and other forms of harassment at school, at work and in the neighborhood. Today, more subtle and sophisticated means are used to discourage emigration. To avoid the difficulties that follow a legal application to emigrate, some Cubans attempt to leave clandestinely and illegally. Others do so after effectively being denied permission to leave.

The C-8 form letter

Critics of the government have often waited for years for permission to emigrate. Many Cubans who are critical of the government, or who are former political prisoners, have been essentially denied permission to emigrate in a form-letter known as the C-8, which is issued by the Ministry of Interior's Department of Immigration and Foreign Affairs. The C-8 states: "it is not pos-

---

1   Organization of Americas States Inter-American Commission on Human Rights, The Situation of Human Rights in Cuba, Seventh Report, October 1983.

sible to grant authorization [of your request] because it does not correspond to any established emigration provisions." It continues, "We will notify you should there be a change that would make a favorable solution possible ...." Until the C-8 is rescinded, its bearer is barred from leaving the country. Although the C-8 is not an outright rejection of permission to emigrate, which could be easily identified as a blatant violation of freedom of movement standards, it effectively postpones indefinitely departure from the country.

Cubans with no record of political opposition to the government may be subjected to the same form of punishment, especially if they are well-known. Severino Puente Diaz and Lydia Montes Morales received a C-8 from the Ministry of Interior in January 1983, barring them from leaving Cuba. Puente and Montes, who had worked in radio and television for 30 years as writers and actors, had sought to join their children in the U.S. since they were granted visas to enter the U.S. and Spain in 1982.

Puente and Montes were popular entertainers who did not come into conflict with the authorities, and both had good jobs until they expressed the desire to leave Cuba. According to their children, Puente and Montes were relieved of their jobs after the Ministry of Interior informed their superiors of their application to leave the country. Cubans are expected to leave their jobs once they are scheduled to leave the country. Many have spent months or years without a job after their travel plans went awry or after they were prevented from leaving. While nothing prevented Puentes and Montes from looking for new jobs, no one would hire them in radio or TV. Puente, who is 58, eventually took a job in agriculture, but medical problems later prevented him from keeping the job.

In addition to enduring minor harassment by strangers, on several occasions they have been summoned to state security headquarters for questioning. In March 1988, Puente and Montes joined Ricardo Bofill's Cuban Committee for Human Rights. In June, they received permission to leave the country after a certain amount of U.S. press attention was brought to their case, and now reside in the U.S.

Judging by what seems to have been a recent policy reversal toward members of the Cuban Committee for Human Rights (CCPDH), it seems the decision to rescind a C-8 is based, at least in part, on arbitrary and perhaps political considerations. Less than two weeks after the acrimonious media campaign launched against Bofill and the CCPDH, eighteen members of the Committee, many of whom had C-8 forms, were granted permission to leave the country, most after years of failed efforts, all within a month of the United Nations Commission on Human Rights meeting in Geneva at which it was agreed to send a delegation to Cuba. Others affiliated with CCPDH or the Cuban Commission for Human Rights and National Reconciliation (CCPDHRN) have been repeatedly denied permission to leave in the past. However, in addition to granting the CCPDH members permission to leave in early 1988, the Cuban government granted Elizardo Sánchez, leader of CCDHRN, permission to visit his wife and children in Miami, and permitted him to return at the end of three and a half months. Sánchez is the first self-described human rights monitor to be permitted to leave and to return to Cuba. We applaud this step by the Cuban government and urge that this right should be granted to all Cubans in a non-discriminatory manner. We note, however, that in December 1988, Sánchez was denied permission to travel to Spain to attend a human rights conference.

Seeking political asylum outside Cuba and consequences

José Alberto Menéndez Suárez, a trainer for the national Cuban cycling team, travelled to Panama in December 1987 for an international competition. When he was asked by the Panamanians to stay on to assist them with their cycling program, he requested permission from his superior in Cuba. Menéndez's request was turned down and they had an argument. Fearing retaliation in his job when he returned home, Menéndez decided not to go back. He obtained political asylum in the U.S. Embassy.

Reprisals were taken against Menéndez's wife and son in Cuba. After he claimed asylum, his wife, Emma Carmona de Lázaro, 25, was detained at least four times by state security police, according to Menéndez. She had to give up her job when she applied to leave Cuba to join her husband. Both Emma Carmona and her son were denied permission to leave Cuba until September 1988, and then only after Menéndez had brought a considerable amount of international and press attention to their case.

45

Juana Hilda García del Monte has been waiting for permission to emigrate for eight years. Her husband, Dr. Guillermo del Monte, a physician, obtained political asylum in Newfoundland in 1980 while en route to Congo where he was to perform obligatory medical service for the second time, against his will. He now lives in Canada. The Cuban government has repeatedly refused to allow his wife to leave Cuba.

Another case that has recently come to Americas Watch's attention is that of Paquito D'Rivera, an internationally celebrated saxophonist, whose 13-year old son and ex-wife have been trying to emigrate for eight years. D'Rivera obtained political asylum in Spain during a concert tour in 1980.

Pedro Pablo Sosa Ortega, 20 years old at the time, attempted to obtain political asylum in Shannon, Ireland on January 21, 1987 when the Cubana Airlines plane he was on was forced to land due to mechanical difficulties. Sosa was on his way from Cuba to East Germany to resume participation in a government work program. His request for asylum was communicated both to Irish authorities and to the U.S. Embassy in Dublin. According to Irish authorities, Sosa was denied asylum in Ireland on the grounds that he did not qualify under the 1951 U.N. Convention on the Status of Refugees. He was not granted asylum in the U.S., according to the U.S. State Department, because it was given less than two hours to respond to his plea.

Sosa was detained upon his return to Cuba and taken to "Villa Marista," the state security facility in Havana. He was held there for one month during which he was subjected to psychologically disorienting treatment (See Chapter 6, "Detention Procedures"). Sosa was then released on parole.

Sosa was tried in July 1987 on charges of "abandoning public duties" (Article 135 of the current penal code) for shirking his obligation to the work program in East Germany. He was defended by an attorney whose defense consisted of asking that the charge should be changed to the lesser crime of "illegal exit," (salida ilegal Article 216) and asking the court to have mercy on her client since he was so young. Sosa was sentenced to three years in prison under Article 135. But before he was imprisoned, in August, Sosa attempted to leave the country illegally in an inner tube. Sosa was caught, re-arrested, held in Villa Marista for two weeks and then taken to La Cabaña prison in Havana where he

46

was held from August 27 to January 21, 1988. He was re-sentenced to an additional 1 1/2 years in prison for salida ilegal.

According to Sosa, who now resides in the U.S., in La Cabaña, just in his galley, there were as many as twenty who had attempted to leave the country illegally, most on rafts. Sosa also met others in separate galleys who were arrested for *salida ilegal*, and estimated that there were ten to twenty prisoners who had tried to leave the country illegally in each of the fifteen galleys in his zone. In his galley, he says, there were three young men who were detained for having *talked* about seeking asylum in the Embassy of Venezuela. They were reportedly held without trial for one year and then released.

After his second trial in January 1988, Sosa was transferred to Combinado del Este prison, where he was again held with common prisoners. In his cell block, which held between thirty and forty prisoners, twelve were imprisoned for *salida ilegal*.

Sosa was released from prison on May 23, 1988, prior to the completion of his sentence, due to efforts on his behalf by an Irish lawyer, among others. One week later, on May 31, when Sosa was to have an immigration interview at the U.S. Interests Section in Havana, he was summoned to appear at a local police station. He was told his case of "abandoning public duties" was still pending and he was threatened with reimprisonment and detained overnight. The next day he was taken back to La Cabaña; his head was shaved and he was given a prison uniform. That evening he was again released. He continued to be harassed by the police -- he would be summoned to the police station, or several police would check on him at home -- until he was permitted to leave Cuba and flew to the U.S. on August 5, 1988.

Cuban exiles arrested during visits to Cuba

Orestes Rafael González Fernández, a U.S. permanent resident since 1973, visited Cuba in November 1981 to see his son and his father; the latter had suffered a heart attack. Four days after his arrival, González was arrested in his son's home. He was detained for 6 months, tried and sentenced to twenty years in prison for allegedly belonging to Alpha 66, a militant anti-Castro exile group,

47

and for his alleged "counterrevolutionary activities." He is being held in Combinado del Este prison. His son was detained for one month.

Inquiries by the U.S. Interests Section have elicited little information from the Cuban government, since González is a Cuban citizen and the Cuban government is not required to provide information on his case. Given the denial of information to the family in the United States, it is not possible for Americas Watch to determine whether there was evidence presented against González of participation in activity that could warrant the charges and conviction.

Nicolas Raúl Valladares, a Cuban-born naturalized U.S. citizen, visited Cuba in January 1987 to see his ailing father, according to information provided to Americas Watch by Representative Howard Berman's (D. California) office. He was an employee of a cousin of Representative Berman in Los Angeles. Valladares was due to leave Cuba on January 25. After being dropped off at the Havana airport by his brother, Valladares was reportedly arrested and accused of espionage. In response to inquiries about his case in June 1987, Representative Berman was informed by the Cuban Interests Section in Washington that Valladares had committed suicide in his cell the previous month by hanging himself with a shirt and towel.

Influence of U.S.-Cuban relations

The resumption of an immigration agreement between the U.S. and Cuba could do much to reduce the number of Cubans who attempt to leave illegally. Normal immigration between the U.S. and Cuba was last halted in May 1985 when the U.S. began broadcasting to Cuba over Radio Martí and Cuba responded by abrogating the agreement. Under the renewed immigration agreement of November 1987, up to 20,000 Cubans will be able to emigrate to the U.S. from Cuba or from "third countries" such as Venezuela, Panama and Costa Rica, and up to 3,000 more, mainly former political prisoners, will be able to enter the U.S. with refugee status annually. In return, Cuba will accept the return of approximately 2,700 excludable Cuban detainees who arrived in the U.S. in 1980 in the Mariel Boatlift.

In the first year of the renewed agreement, approximately 2,500 former prisoners and family members entered the U.S. with refugee status. Beginning in early 1988, approximately 400 visas per month have been issued by the U.S. Interests Section to Cubans seeking to emigrate. Five Mariel detainees were deported to Cuba in December 1988 and, at this writing, another nine deportations are pending.[2]

In November 1988, the Cuban government lifted some restrictions on travel to Cuba by exiles in the U.S. Under this measure, a number of Cuban-born exiles who emigrated prior to 1978, as well as U.S.-born children under the age of 25 of that group of exiles, will be permitted to visit Cuba.

Illegal Exit

Gustavo and Sebastian Arcos Bergnes were released from Combinado del Este prison in March 1988 and May 1987 respectively after serving sentences for "*salida ilegal del pais*" (illegal exit from the country). Gustavo Arcos had been a prominent revolutionary figure, having participated in the assault on the Moncada Barracks with Fidel Castro in 1953. Under Castro he served as Ambassador to Belgium, Luxemburg, Denmark and Iceland. Sebastian Arcos, a dentist, who was also active in the fight against Batista, held several positions in the Ministry of Finance, then served in the Navy as a dentist and later practiced dentistry under the Ministry of Public Health.

In 1979, during a period of improved relations between the U.S. and Cuba, Gustavo, who had been imprisoned for several years in the 1960s for his open criticism of the government and then served one year of a ten-year sentence for "crimes against the powers of the State," applied to emigrate but was denied permission by the Cuban government. In December of that year, Gustavo heard that his son who was living in Miami was in a coma following a car

---

2   Americas Watch has been critical of United States treatment of the Mariel detainees. Our continuing objections to their treatment were discussed most recently in "The Reagan Administration's Record on Human Rights in 1988," published in January 1989, at pp. 324-325 of the press edition.

accident. For the next two years, Gustavo was repeatedly denied permission to leave. In December 1981, Gustavo, Sebastian and Sebastian Jr. were caught attempting to leave clandestinely from La Habana del Este on a fishing boat.

Gustavo was sentenced to and served seven years in prison; Sebastian was sentenced to and served six years; and Sebastian Jr. was sentenced to and served one year on charges of *salida ilegal* and "trafficking in foreign currency" for being in possession of U.S. currency. In addition, Sebastian Jr. was expelled from the university.

Both Gustavo and Sebastian are members of the Cuban Committee for Human Rights. Shortly after his release in March 1988, Gustavo, as well as Sebastian, were summoned to the Department of Immigration and Foreign Affairs along with other CCPDH members to receive permission to emigrate. In May, they were once again denied permission, however. Sebastian Jr. received a C-8 letter from the Ministry of Interior also in May. The three continue to wait for the Cuban government to allow them to leave.

Juan Morina and his brother José Antonio Morina were imprisoned in July 1980 and each was sentenced to five years in prison for attempting to leave the country illegally. They were initially held in La Cabaña prison and then transferred to Nieves Morejón prison. Soon after they were placed in Nieves Morejon, they were both seriously wounded in a clash between prisoners and guards. Their prison terms were more than doubled as a result of this episode, making each required to serve a total of thirteen years.

Pedro Pablo Morejón García, 25, was sentenced to a three-year prison term in 1980 for attempting to leave the country illegally. While in prison, he was accused of committing a homicide, he says falsely, and sentenced to an additional 13 years. Morejón, a teacher of Spanish literature, is being held in Boniato prison in Santiago de Cuba. His family lives in Havana.

Armando Ortiz González, a 25-year-old student, was arrested and sentenced in 1982 to eight years in prison for attempting to leave the country illegally. He was held in Combinado del Este prison until mid-1987, when he was transferred to a work camp (*granja*). Three years were added to his original sentence when he was caught trying to escape from the *granja*, and he was returned to Combinado del Este prison. In April 1988, he was transferred again to another *granja*. He was granted early release in May 1988.

Gustavo Martínez Jiménez, a leader of JARPE, (see Chapter 2, "Freedom of Association and Assembly") was sentenced to fifteen years in prison in 1980, for attempting to leave the country illegally. He is currently imprisoned in the Van Troi work camp.

Seeking Political Asylum in Foreign Embassies in Havana

The Embassy of Peru

In April 1980, more than 10,000 Cubans sought asylum in the Peruvian Embassy in Havana, initiating the exodus that would come to be known as the "Mariel Boatlift." It began on April 1 when a group of Cubans stormed through the Embassy gates in a bus. One Cuban guard died during the incident, though it is unclear whether he was run over by the bus or whether he was hit in the crossfire after several guards opened fired on the asylum-seekers. The Peruvians offered refuge to the Cubans and did not hand them over to the Cuban authorities. Three days later, the Cuban government announced that it would remove its guards from the Embassy in order not to risk the lives of additional Cuban guards. Within days, the grounds of the Embassy of Peru were filled to capacity with Cubans seeking to leave the country. Over half of those who sought asylum in the Embassy in 1980, were eventually accepted by the governments of the U.S., Peru, Spain, Costa Rica, Canada, Ecuador and Belgium.[3]

Three persons, however, have remained inside the Embassy for eight years, waiting for the Peruvian and Cuban governments to resolve their request to leave Cuba. They entered the Embassy of Peru on April 5, the day after Cuban guards were withdrawn. All three had previously been denied permission to

---

3   Organization of American States Inter-American Commission of Human Rights, The Situation of Human Rights in Cuba, Seventh Report, October 1983.

leave the country reportedly because they had served or worked for the Cuban armed forces.

According to a letter they addressed to the Cuban exile press in 1986, they identify themselves as:

Felino Ramírez Batista, 56, heavy machinery operator, fought against Batista in the Sierra Maestra and served as a personal bodyguard to Castro during the first 2 years of the revolution. He left the army in 1962.

Eduardo Herrera Díaz, 38, worked as a civilian electrician at a military installation for 9 months.

Pedro Betancourt Collazo, 28, carpenter, cut cane as a member of the Youth Labor Army, which is obligatory. He is considered a deserter.

Thirty-two asylum-seekers remained in the Peruvian Embassy after 1980. All except Ramírez, Herrera and Betancourt had accepted "amnesties" offered by the Cuban government over the years, permitting them to return to their homes without reprisals. There is concern that reprisals have been taken against some of them. In June 1988, EFE, the Spanish news agency, reported that an agreement had been reached between Havana and Lima that would allow the three remaining asylees to be taken from the embassy directly to the airport and flown to Peru sometime in the next six months. At present, they remain in the embassy.[4]

The Papal Nunciature

In December 1980, three months after the port of Mariel was closed, a group of Cubans forcibly entered the Papal nunciature in Havana, and reportedly took hostages in an attempt to obtain safe conduct out of Cuba. Within ten minutes, Cuban authorities responded by surrounding the premises. Four hours later, Cuban police broke through the windows of the building and the

---

4   Another man has remained in the Embassy of Venezuela since 1980. Not much is known about his case, however.

asylum seekers were detained. An employee of the nunciature died during the incident. Americas Watch has been unable to verify reports that some of the participants were armed and took hostages.

At least three people were executed in connection with this incident. According to their mother, the three brothers, Cipriano, 22, Eugenio, 26, and Ventura García Marín, 28, were executed in La Cabaña in January 1981. Cipriano García Marín had previously served a two-year sentence between 1977-79 for attempting to leave the country illegally on a Greek ship. Their mother, Margarita Marín Thompson, a woman in her 60s who entered the nunciature with her sons, was charged with violating "the right of extra-territoriality" and was sentenced to twenty-five years in prison but served only six years in Nuevo Amanecer prison and the women's prison outside Havana (*Centro de Reeducación de Mujeres de Occidente*). Eumelia Pérez Arias, the widow of Eugenio García Marín, was imprisoned for one year from December 25, 1980 to December 24, 1981.

Samuel Hernández Reyes, 34, was sentenced to twenty-five years in prison in 1980 on charges of violating "the right of extra-territoriality" for entering the Papal nunciature and is currently held in Combinado del Este prison. He had been previously detained several times under the "dangerousness" provisions, Articles 72-90 of the current penal code. Hernández is a member of CCPDH in prison.

Alfredo Jiménez Ramos, student, was sentenced to twenty-five years in prison in 1980 in connection with his attempt to enter the Papal nunciature. He is currently being held in Combinado del Este. Jiménez collaborates with CCPDH in prison.

The Embassy of Ecuador

On February 13, 1981, two families forcibly entered the Ecuadoran Embassy seeking to leave the country. According to our information, they were not armed. The fourteen individuals remained in the Embassy one week expecting to obtain safe-conduct out of the country. At the end of the week, on a Friday, the Ecuadoran Ambassador, Jorge Pérez Concha, left the Embassy for the weekend promising to return on Monday to make arrangements for their safe-conduct. On Saturday, February 21, Cuban police surrounded the Embassy and forced out the asylum-seekers. Windows were broken, and tear gas thrown in. Some walked out of the Embassy because they were choking, other were forcibly removed. According to eyewitnesses the scene was chaotic and violent. Those who were wounded were treated -- stitches, oxygen -- in a hospital, before being taken to Villa Marista.

One of those who had sought refuge at the Embassy was a 15-year old boy, Juan Owen Delgado Temprana, who had a history of medical problems. He was reportedly wounded and was brought to a military hospital before being sent home, and died shortly thereafter -- eighteen days after being removed from the premises of the Embassy. The Cuban government has attempted to refute allegations that it is responsible for the death of Owen. In the February 14, 1988 edition of *Granma*, the government claims the boy suffered a head injury while playing with his brother at the home of their grandmother, subsequent to the Embassy incident, and died at the Pinar del Río provincial hospital as a result of respiratory failure.

The others were held in Villa Marista for five months. Though they were not physically mistreated, they were frequently interrogated in the middle of the night about the others involved, who else knew of their plans, etc. At first, they were held in separate cells, but eventually they were moved to cells with three to seven others. One month into detention, a mother and daughter were placed in a cell together after the daughter tried to commit suicide.

They asked that a relative, Domingo Jorge Delgado Fernández, take up their defense, but they were not given access to counsel while they were in state security detention. Delgado was not present at the trial either. He had been arrested before the trial took place.

Domingo Jorge Delgado Fernández, 43, a lawyer, worked as a legal adviser at the provincial level for the Ministry of Public Health in Pinar del Río, where he was born, and was President of the Bahía Honda Municipal Court until 1981. Delgado immediately attempted to take on the defense of the group, upon learning of their detention. Several days later, on February 23 or 24, he was detained for a few days. In the course of preparing a defense, he visited the Ecuadoran Embassy on several occasions to interview its staff. On December

25, 1981 Delgado, himself was arrested and although he had not attempted to enter the Embassy with the others, he was charged with the same crime, violating the "right of extra-territoriality," Article 249 of the 1979 penal code. Degaldo served almost 6 1/2 years of an eight-year prison sentence before his release in May 1988.

Four acquaintances from their neighborhood reportedly stood trial along with those who actually entered the Embassy. The lawyer appointed to handle their case never met with the defendants before the trial, and virtually the only defense he put up was to ask that the court take into consideration that many of the defendants were young. No witnesses were called on their behalf. Though they had requested that Ecuadoran Ambassador Pérez attend the trial, he was not present. The trial lasted from 8:00 am to 9:00 or 10:00 pm, with a one-hour break for lunch, and a fifteen-minute recess in the afternoon.

They were charged with "other acts against the security of the State," Articles 132-136; "acts that affect the right of extra-territoriality," Article 249; and "acts against heads and diplomatic representatives of foreign states," Article 119 of the 1979 penal code. The young people (16-18 years old) were sentenced to fifteen years in prison; the men were sentenced to thirty years in prison; the women were sentenced to twenty years in prison. One person who attempted but did not actually succeed in entering the Embassy was sentenced to eight years. The following are those currently serving sentences or who recently were released in this case:

Mercedes Benita Balanza, a woman in her 50s, is serving a twenty-year prison term in the women's prison in Havana (*Centro de Reeducacion para Mujeres del Occidente*).

Maria Elena Moreno Balanza, approximately 24 years old, daughter of Mercedes Benita Balanza, is serving a fifteen-year prison term in the women's prison in Havana.

Lazaro Omar Moreno Balanza, 25 son of Mercedes Benita Balanza, is serving a fifteen-year prison term in Combinado del Este.

Gilberto Mario Moreno Balanza, son of Mercedes Benita Balanza, is imprisoned in Van Troi work camp.

Rolando Felix Camejo Loaces, is believed to be serving a 43-year prison term in Combinado del Este.

Pascual Ovidio Delgado Fernández is serving a 45-year prison sentence in Combinado del Este.

Romulo Juan Delgado Fernández is serving a 45-year prison sentence in Combinado del Este.

Sergio Alvarado Fumero, Leonel Blanco Peña, Carlos Manuel Marquez Rodríguez, Elsa Temprana, Jorge Rafael Delgado Fernández, have completed or have been released prior to completion of their sentences. Reylan and German Delgado Temprana were detained briefly at the time of the incident and later released.

Those in the case who have been granted early release and their families, as well as family members of those still in prison, have endured a precarious existence. Most are still waiting to leave Cuba, but have had difficulty obtaining visas. As recently as the first week of August 1988, German Delgado, the son of Romulo Juan Delgado, was fired from his job in a tile factory when he asked for time off to visit his father in prison.

It seems that the Cuban government deals as harshly as it does with those who attempt to leave the country because it is not only an embarrassment but also it has been perceived as a threat to the revolution. In the early years of the Castro government, leaving the country illegally was seen as an attempt to aid enemies of the revolution from abroad and could carry severe punishment imposed by the Revolutionary Tribunals. The Mariel boatlift, during which approximately 125,000 Cubans fled the country in 1980 seeking civil and political freedom or economic opportunity on the soil of Cuba's arch-enemy, was a great blow to the "prestige" of the revolution two decades later.

The Cuban government maintains that those involved in the Ecuadoran Embassy case were not persecuted and thus defamed the state by seeking asylum.

Americas Watch recognizes that the Cuban government has an obligation to protect diplomats and diplomatic compounds. Moreover, Americas Watch does not condone the use of violence in seeking political asylum. Whether or to what extent force was used in some of these cases is not entirely clear to us. We present these cases, however, to show the desperation of some Cubans who have not been able to obtain legal permission to emigrate or who fear reprisals if they seek to emigrate legally.

Indications that emigration restrictions continue to provoke Cubans who wish to leave the country to flock to the embassies in Havana were evident as recently as May and June 1987. An undetermined number of visa-seekers gathered outside the French Embassy after hearing a rumor that the French government was prepared to grant visas to those who wanted to leave Cuba, and several dozen were arrested. The rumor was apparently based on an interview with Fidel Castro that was published in the French Communist newspaper, *L'Humanité*, in which Castro declared, "We are willing to let go all those who want to leave, if France gives them a visa."[5]

Many were reportedly detained briefly. However, at least one individual, Lorenzo Dueñas, was reportedly sentenced to two years in prison on charges of violating "the right of extra-territoriality," and is believed to be held in Combinado del Este prison.

In May 1987, a man believed to be called Jesus Rodríguez attempted to forcibly enter the U.S. Interests Section and was sentenced to 2 1/2 years in prison on charges of violating "the right of extra-territoriality." He is currently in Combinado del Este prison.

In October 1988, one woman and two men entered the official residence of the Ambassador of West Germany seeking refuge. According to our information, they were unarmed. They remained inside for three days, and then left willingly with assurances from the West German officials that the Cuban authorities agreed not to take reprisals against them. They were reportedly detained shortly thereafter, along with another man who had attempted but had not succeeded in entering the Ambassador's residence. Although it has been difficult to verify the status of their cases, we have received reports that

---

5   Meluza, Lourdes, "Visa-seekers are arrested in Havana," The Miami Herald, June 12, 1987.

they were held for some time in Villa Marista and the woman is now believed to be held in the Havana women's prison; the men in Combinado del Este prison. They are awaiting trial. They are said to be Xiomara Pérez González, Hermohenes Pérez Díaz, Juan Antonio Morera Dorta and Roberto Arteaga Rodríguez.

PRIVACY AND SURVEILLANCE

Committees for the Defense of the Revolution

The right to privacy proclaimed in Article 12 of the Universal Declaration of Human Rights may well be the most systematically violated human right in Cuba today. Almost every aspect of the lives of Cubans is monitored by neighborhood surveillance groups known as Committees for the Defense of the Revolution (CDR). These groups are also empowered to intervene, forcibly if necessary, to prevent or stop any suspect activity or behavior. The CDRs were created, according to a recent Cuban radio commentary, "with the sacred mission of defending the revolution and blocking the political action of its enemies. Revolutionary vigilance was and continues to be their essential mission and reason for being."[1]

The CDRs, which celebrated the 28th anniversary of their formation in September 1988, are responsible for observing and reporting to a variety of government ministries and organizations the political and ideological conduct of residents of each block. Cubans must receive the approval of their CDRs to obtain day care for their children, to be admitted to university or to change jobs, to cite a few examples of their reach. Through their vigilance, CDRs control the behavior of those they monitor.

---

1   FBIS-LAT, April 15, 1988.

The presence of CDRs is pervasive. In 1983, according to one estimate, five million Cubans were members of CDRs, out of the general population of about ten million.[2] By 1986, the number of members of the organization was announced at 6,662,568.[3] According to the Cuban radio station Radio Reloj in September 1987, there were over 800 CDR "zones" and over 400,000 CDR members in the province[4] of Havana alone, which has a population of about 2,000,000. A sign by the door or window of at least one house on nearly every block marks the presence of a Committee.

In early 1988, a reduction in the report-filing responsibilities of the CDRs was announced. The reports on "the attitude and behavior of their neighbors,"[5] routinely submitted by CDRs upon request by Cuban authorities, and known as the "I certify" (*hago constar*), were to be made available only to certain government offices. Now, according to the Cuban press, only the Communist Party and the Communist Youth Union may solicit information on a person's upbringing; only the State Committee of Labor and Social Security may request information with regard to pensions, economic aid and young people who wish to qualify to live abroad in other socialist countries; and only the Ministry of Justice may solicit information with respect to the cancellation of criminal records and the election of lay judges. All the information submitted to authorities is now to be public though what this means has not been made,

---

2   Hoyt Williams, John, "Havana's Military Machine," The Atlantic, August 1988.

3   Ibid.

4   FBIS-LAT, October 2, 1987.

5   Sosa, Diana, "Suspenden entregas de Hago Constar en los CDR," Granma, June 28, 1988.

completely clear. It may mean that the subjects of reports will be informed about requests for information about them, as well as about the substance of the information provided. The reason given for these changes in the use of the hago constar reports was that "on the one hand, [it] has been unnecessarily requested by many organs and institutions, and on the other hand, has generated problems and complaints by neighbors since the information has not been correct in all cases.[6]

Among the other documentation that has been available to Cuban authorities is the *boleta recogida de opiniones*,[7] a form on which to record the opinions of others, used by the CDRs. On one side of the form there is a blank space for the text of the remark and a line at the bottom for the name of the person completing the form. The other side requires information about the speaker: age, sex, occupation, "integration" ("revolutionary, disaffected, unknown"), the place where the comment was made (at work, school, home, street, commercial center, recreational center, transport), and the reaction by listeners (approval, disapproval, indifference).

Throughout 1988 the CDRs were urged by members of the Central Committee of the Communist Party to "confront problems in the community, through greater political and ideological work [and] increased revolutionary combativeness and vigilance."[8] The call for increased combativeness is cause for alarm since the role of the CDRs is not limited to monitoring and reporting; according to Radio Reloj they have a "moral responsibility to confront any anti-

---

6   Ibid.

7   A defender of the Cuban government's human rights record, Prof. Debra Evenson of DePaul University Law School, asserts that this boleta was not used after 1980. Letter to The New York Review of Books, October 13, 1988.

8   Sosa, Diana, "Modificaciones en el trabajo y estructura de los CDR," Granma, March 25, 1988.

social behavior."[9] In carrying out this part of their work, the CDRs are responsible for some of the most violent acts of repression in recent Cuban history.

In 1980 when more than 120,000 Cubans left Cuba through the port of Mariel, the CDRs were given license to vent their hostility against those who sought to emigrate (See Chapter 3, "Freedom of Movement"). The CDRs were permitted to unleash a campaign of severe beatings by mobs of government supporters in the street, stone-throwing, vandalism and besieging of homes, verbal abuse and harassment of workers at their jobs and children at their schools. The campaign lasted several weeks.

Such so-called "acts of repudiation" have not ceased altogether, however. In 1988, Americas Watch received reports of several incidents of severe harassment of human rights activists by the CDRs (See Chapter 2, "Freedom of Association and Assembly").

The Ministry of Education also participates in political surveillance by keeping records on students' views from pre-school through university. The *expediente acumulativo del escolar* is the log-book which documents information about each child, such as names of parents, medical record and scholastic aptitude. In addition, the *expediente* contains information on the "ideological integration" of the parents; whether the family participates actively in religion; and under the section "ideological, political and moral education," a teacher may comment that the student was removed from the Communist Youth Union or whether the student's remarks have a sound political base.

Americas Watch objects strenuously to the CDRs' license to inform secretly on their neighbors' political and ideological beliefs and the potentially harmful results. An individual may never obtain a job promotion, or admission to a school, or the right to travel based on a CDR report without knowing what he did wrong and without recourse. Recent changes in the operations of the CDRs do not reflect a fundamental change in the nature of the system. In spite

---

9   FBIS-LAT, August 24, 1988.

of the reduction in the number of reports the CDRs are required to submit, it is doubtful that surveillance and its harmful consequences will diminish if the Communist Party, the Communist Youth Union, the State Committee on Labor and Social Security and the Ministry of Justice continue to expect to be kept informed about the attitudes and behavior of all Cubans so as to make decisions about their lives.

Americas Watch also objects to the role of the CDRs as civilian patrols that have the authority of the government to single out those holding "counter-revolutionary" opinions or conducting politically suspect activities, and to assault them physically or verbally. Whether the violent acts committed by the CDRs have been explicitly ordered or whether they have been spontaneous, the Castro government has condoned this extra-legal harassment of dissenters, and the victims have no legal recourse.

"Dangerousness"

Articles 72-90 of the current penal code define behavior that is considered "dangerous" and provide for the application of security measures to prevent crimes by dangerous people who conduct themselves in a manner that contradicts "socialist morality." The application of these provisions is based on Cuba's strict system of surveillance.

"Indications of dangerousness" include habitual drunkenness, alcoholism, drug-addiction and "anti-social behavior." The last is defined as the habitual disturbance of social co-existence through violent or provocative acts, violation of the rights of others, living like a "social parasite" from the labor of others, or practicing socially unacceptable vices. A person in a dangerous state may receive a warning from the police; the warning is to be made in the form of a document describing the activity considered dangerous, as well as the response of the person in question and his signature.

Medidas de seguridad pre-delictivas are security measures applied before the crime is committed; *medidas de seguridad post-delictivas* are measures applied after the crime is committed. The first consists of therapeutic measures such as medical, psychiatric or detoxification assistance until recovery; re-educational measures such as internment in an establishment specializing in work or study for one to four years; and surveillance by the police for one to four years. The second may be applied to the mentally ill who cannot be responsible for themselves; those who become mentally ill while serving a prison sentence; alcoholics or drug-addicts who commit crimes; recidivists who commit a breach of a court order.

Americas Watch is concerned that "the state of dangerousness" remains in the new criminal code. In the past it has been used to punish peaceful critics of the government. Americas Watch is concerned that the preventive detention provision may be used against anyone the government considers "antisocial," including human rights activists (see Chapter 2, "Freedom of Association and Assembly"); and that other "dangerousness" provisions serve to justify occasional "visits" to their homes by state security police. Although we know of no recent use of the *post-delictiva* measure, in the past it has been used to prolong prison sentences or to re-sentence defiant political prisoners.

Correspondence

Article 56 of the Cuban Constitution states that "correspondence is inviolable. It can be seized, opened and examined only in cases prescribed by law." The same principle applies to cable, telegraph and telephone communications. This consitutional guarantee is protected by Article 289 and 290 of the current penal code (formerly Articles 343 and 344). Opening another person's letter, telegram, cable or other correspondence, or listening to a private phone call, or revealing the contents of these constitutes a "violation of the privacy of correspondence" and is punishable by three months to one year in prison -- formerly three to nine months. If a government official or public servant commits this crime, the penalty which had been six months to three years in prison, has been reduced to six months to two years in the new penal code.

Nevertheless, several cases that have come to the attention of Americas Watch indicate not only that mail, especially to and from abroad, is monitored closely, but also that the content of supposedly inviolable correspondence may be construed as enemy propaganda and may lead to imprisonment. Americas Watch knows of no convictions for violation of the privacy of correspondence.

The following cases illustrate the way that the right to privacy has been violated in Cuba:

- Pascual Andrés Hernández Murguía, a teacher, was arrested in 1982 and sentenced to 6 years in prison for sending letters abroad and having conversations in which he expressed opinions critical of the Cuban government. Hernández was released in June 1986.

- Rafael Lanza López was arrested in 1982 and sentenced to 8 years in prison for sending letters to various embassies in Havana, including the residence of the Papal Nuncio. The letters were reportedly critical of the Cuban government. He was released from Combinado del Este prison in July 1988.

- Gregorio Peña Estrabao was arrested in 1982 and sentenced to 8 years in prison for receiving a letter from the U.S. containing press clippings attacking the Cuban government. Peña had previously served two years of a four-year sentence for attempting to leave the country illegally. He was released from Las Tunas prison in Oriente province in late 1987.

- Andrés Solares Teseiro, a civil engineer, was arrested in 1981 and sentenced to 8 years for planning to organize an opposition political party and for intending to send letters requesting advice to President Francois Mitterand and Senator Edward Kennedy. Solares was reportedly held in a punishment cell for one year, from late 1984 to late 1985. He was released from Combinado del Este prison in May 1988 and flown directly to the U.S.

House Search

The state security police have been known to conduct searches in the homes of peaceful dissenters, such as writers or human rights activists. The house searches have led to arrests on charges of enemy propaganda if books, manuscripts or letters that were critical of the government were found; or detention without charge for varying lengths of time until as recently as September

65

1986 (See Chapter 2, "Freedom of Association and Assembly"). Articles 215-240 of the Law of Criminal Procedure provide for house search, as well as searches of books and documents, and opening of correspondence when there is reason to believe these may yield evidence against the suspect. Under these provisions, an *instructor*, who is not a magistrate, is empowered to issue search warrants. Americas Watch condemns these practices when they are used as a means to harass, intimidate or imprison peaceful critics of the government.

It is worth pointing out that we did not received complaints of searches in the homes of human rights activists during 1988, though as this report goes to press, we received a disturbing report of a house search in January 1989.[10] Nevertheless, we continue to receive complaints about occasional "visits" by agents of the state security police to the homes of human rights activists and ex-political prisoners.

Telephone Communication

Although Americas Watch has managed to maintain almost weekly telephone contact with human rights monitors in Cuba, often the calls are cut off after the connection is made. We assume their telephones are tapped and controlled, and yet it is difficult to ascribe difficulties in communication to anything other than the poor state of the Cuban telephone system. Nevertheless,

---

10   Americas Watch has received reports that four members of a family connected with the Cuban Human Rights Party were detained on January 23. They are Manuel González Jr., Isis Pérez Montes de Oca, Lidia González; and the son of Manuel González and Isis Pérez, Cristian González, who is a small child, was taken to the Havana police station with the others at the time of their arrest. The father of Manuel González was detained on January 24. Manuel González Sr., Lidia González and Manuel González Jr. were tried in a municipal court on the 26th on charges of "clandestine printing" and are now serving prison terms of one year, six months and three months respectively. They had no defense counsel at their trial. (See Chapter 5, "Due Process," footnote 9) Their home, which was searched and items confiscated, is said to be used as the offices of the Human Rights Party. Isis Pérez was reportedly fined and released.

we have reason to believe that occasionally our calls have been interrupted on the orders of Cuban authorities.

DUE PROCESS

Article 58 of the Constitution states:

Nobody may be tried or sentenced except by a competent court by virtue of laws existing prior to the crime and with the formalities and guarantees that the laws establish.

Every accused person has the right to a defense.

No violence or pressure of any kind may be used against people to force them to testify.

All statements obtained in violation of the above precept are null and void, and those responsible shall be punished as prescribed by law.

As written, Article 58 is unobjectionable. Americas Watch is concerned, however, that the rights and guarantees established in Article 58 are violated in practice. Moreover, the lack of an independent judiciary in Cuba, and the absence of a professional commitment by Cuban lawyers to act in the best interests of their clients, renders these guarantees meaningless. In order to clarify Americas Watch's concerns with respect to due process in Cuba, it is useful to examine the Cuban judiciary under international standards and to examine the organization of the Cuban legal profession.

The Judiciary

Article 10 of the Universal Declaration of Human Rights provides that "Everyone is entitled in full equality to a fair trial and public hearing by an independent and impartial tribunal, in the determination of his rights and obligations and of any criminal charge against him."

In addition the U.N. General Assembly has endorsed "Basic Principles on the Independence of the Judiciary" which provide that:

The independence of the judiciary shall be guaranteed by the State and enshrined in the Constitution or the law of the country.... members of the judiciary are... entitled to freedom of expression, belief, association and assembly; provided, however, that in exercising such rights, judges shall always conduct themselves in such a manner as to preserve... the impartiality and independence of the judiciary.[1]

Cuban law does not ensure an independent judiciary. On the contrary, Article 122 of the Constitution establishes that the courts are "subordinate only to the National Assembly of People's Power and the Council of State." According to Articles 72 and 73 of the Constitution, the National Assembly of People's Power (NAPP)[2] is vested with the power to elect the members of the Council of State, as well as its President, who is also the Head of State and Government -- Fidel Castro. Courts subordinate to such a body can hardly be said to be independent of the executive. Moreover, the Constitution specifies that among the main objectives of the courts are "to uphold and strengthen socialist legality"[3] (Article 123); and the Law of the Organization of the Judicial System requires both professional and lay judges to have "active revolutionary integration" (Articles 66 and 68), raising doubts about the impartiality of the courts.

---

1   "Basic Principles on the Independence of the Judiciary" adopted by the Seventh United Nations Congress on the Prevention of Crime and the Treatment of Offenders, and endorsed by General Assembly resolutions 40/32 of November 29, 1985 and 40/146 of December 13, 1985.

2   The NAPP is the legislative organ of the government. Local Assemblies of People's Power are constituted at the provincial and municipal levels. The NAPP is elected by the Municipal Assemblies of People's Power. See Articles 68, 69 and 100 of the Constitution.

3   Article 12 of the Law of the Organization of the Judicial System states that "Socialist legality is guaranteed in the judicial order by:... 3) the obligation of the courts to interpret and apply laws in a way consistent with socialist principles."

In its report, "Human Rights in Cuba," the Association of the Bar of the City of New York writes that "about 43 percent of Cuba's professional and lay judges are members of the Communist Party with a higher percentage of party members represented on the Supreme Court.... all four of the professional judges on the Supreme Court's military panel, all four professional judges on the state security panel, three of the four professional judges on the labor panel and five of the seven professional judges on the criminal panel are members of the Party."[4] Membership in the Party in Cuba is, of course, not analogous to membership in a political party in the United States. The Party is an elite that exercises actual power, as opposed to the ostensible power exercised by the formal instruments of government. It has its own disciplinary structure and expulsion from the Party has very serious consequences. Members of the Party are expected to act in the interests of the Party. The system is not compatible with the concept of an independent branch of government that serves as a check on the excesses of the other branches of government and, thereby, protects the rights of citizens.

Municipal, provincial and Supreme court cases are heard by a panel of professional and lay judges elected by the Assemblies of People's Power at the corresponding three levels.[5] Professional judges are elected to five-year terms, and lay judges serve terms consisting of two non-consecutive months per year for two and a half years, apart from their regular jobs.[6] Lay judges receive thirty to forty-five days of training and participate in seminars conducted by professional judges.

---

4   Henkin, Alice H., et al., "Human Rights in Cuba:Report Of A Delegation Of The Association Of The Bar Of The City Of New York," Volume 43, No. 7, The Record of The Association of the Bar of the City of New York, 1988.

5   The Law of the Organization of the Judicial System, Articles 74 and 75.

6   The Law of the Organization of the Judicial System, Articles 76 and 77.

The Cuban court system consists of the Supreme Court, provincial courts, municipal courts and military courts. Courts at the national and provincial levels include separate sections for criminal, civil and administrative, labor, and state security law. In addition, the Supreme Court includes a military section that hears appeals from the military court system.

The Attorney General (*Fiscal General de la República*), according to Article 131 of the Constitution, is subordinate to the NAPP and the Council of State. The Attorney General is also a member of the Governing Council of the People's Supreme Court (see also Article 124). The Attorney General and assistant attorneys general are elected by the NAPP (Article 132). Prosecutors in the office of the Attorney General are designated by the Council of State and the Attorney General designates all other provincial and municipal prosecutors. All prosecutors serve five years in office. The Attorney General also oversees a military section, and is responsible for prison inspections and responding to prisoners' complaints of mistreatment.

By itself, the fact the the Attorney General is not independent of the executive is not problematical. But the Attorney General's membership on the Governing Council of the People's Supreme Court may interfere with the independence of the judiciary and, because the Attorney General is subordinate to the NAPP and the Council of State, his judicial role is also subordinate to those bodies.

The Lawyers

In order to practice their profession, lawyers must belong to a *bufete colectivo*, a collective law office under the direction of the National Organization of Bufetes Colectivos, unless they work for a state organ, organization or enterprise.[7] Lawyers are not expected to defend rigorously the interests of their

---

7   The Law of the Organization of the Judicial System, Article 145.

clients. The interests of the client are to be subordinate to those of the state. Indeed, the Provisional Board of Directors of the National Organization of Bufetes Colectivos has suggested that:

> The concept that must not prevail among us is that the best attorney is he who attains the acquittal of his client or places the client's interests above the law and morality. Rather, the best attorney is he who through his actions, talent and ability contributes to the victory of the law and the humanist principles of our justice. This is the foundation of the professional prestige of our attorneys and the only concept recognized and admired by our nation of workers. To depart from this is to identify oneself with those of yesteryear who represented and defended the interests of the exploiting class.[8]

Americas Watch agrees that a lawyer has an ethical responsibility to promote justice. But we believe that the lawyer's effort to defend his client vigorously is also an ethical duty and, in and of itself, does not conflict with his responsibility to uphold justice. The derogatory reference to lawyers who "place the client's interests above the law and morality" is highly objectionable, therefore.

Americas Watch has received numerous reports of deficient defenses in trials of politically-motivated offenses. Former defendants have commented that their lawyers are intimidated by the prosecutor. Often, defendants did not see their lawyers -- court-appointed or of their choosing -- until the trial itself. Many former political prisoners have told us that lawyers are not generally permitted to see their clients in detention in a state security facility like Villa Marista. Attempts are not generally made to establish the innocence of the client. Rather, the defense consists of simply asking for the court's mercy on the grounds that the defendant is young; that the defendant can change his ways; or that the charge should be changed to a lesser crime. Little or no evidence,

---

8   Memorias de la Sesion Constitutiva de la Asamblea General, Organizacion Nacional de Bufetes Colectivos, June 1985.

and often no witnesses, are presented on behalf of the defendant. On the other hand, the prosecutor sometimes provides the only witness to testify at a trial: a state security officer. At the municipal court level, which has jurisdiction over "dangerousness" (and the application of *medidas de seguridad pre-delictivas*) and crimes punishable by up to nine months imprisonment, the participation of a defense attorney "is not indispensable."[9]

In November 1988, Tania Díaz Castro, a human rights activist, was arrested and summarily tried and imprisoned along with her son and daughter-in-law (See Chapter 2, "Freedom of Association and Assmebly"). According to her son, Guillermo Rivas Díaz, who has since been released and now resides in the U.S., they had no defense attorney at their trial in the municipal court of Guanabacoa. When Rivas Díaz asked for a lawyer, he was told by the judge that "counterrevolutionaries" did not have the right to a defense. While they could present no witnesses on their behalf, the prosecution called several Combinado del Este prison guards to testify against the defendants.

---

9   The Law of Criminal Procedure, Article 8 and Article 368. It appears that these courts, in which defendants may be tried without counsel, are now sentencing defendants to up to one year in prison. The law is currently being revised to conform to this practice.

Detention Procedures

Americas Watch has long been concerned with political arrests and imprisonment in Cuba. Cubans detained for politically-motivated offenses have generally been detained by state security police and taken to their nearest post. The best known G-2, or state security facility, is Villa Marista in Havana. Similar facilities are said to be located in each of the provinces. Common prisoners are not taken to state security facilities. Although the Cuban government does not consider those who attempt to leave the country illegally to be political prisoners but rather common criminals, suspects in *salida ilegal* cases are taken to state security facilities.

Though representatives of Americas Watch who visited Cuban prisons in early 1988 were not able to visit Villa Marista, a delegation from Amnesty International was permitted to tour the facility. Amnesty International (AI) describes Villa Marista as having 70 cells, six of which are for women. The men's cells hold four beds each, two beds on each side, one above the other, which fold down from the wall on chains. The women's cells contain single beds and separate bathrooms. At the time of AI's visit, five men were being held at Villa Marista on charges of complicity in attempts to leave the country illegally.[1]

The accounts we have obtained on treatment in these facilities in recent years do not include outright physical torture. On the other hand, they do include such forms of physical and psychological abuse as requiring prisoners to

---

1   According to AI's report, 1,292 people were detained by state security police in 1987, of whom 681 were charged and imprisoned. Of the 681, 574 were arrested for attempting to leave the country illegally. Cuba: Recent Developments Affecting the Situation of Political Prisoners and the Use of the Death Penalty. Amnesty International, September 1988.

stand motionless for periods of several hours; waking them at odd hours for interrogation and sleep deprivation; interrogation consisting of often meaningless or irrelevant questions, sometimes conducted in very cold, air-conditioned
rooms; irregular feeding; isolating detainees in cells by themselves or confining
up to four or more detainees in a cell with little room to move about; artificial
light that is never turned off; and other methods that seem intended to disorient
them and make them pliable under interrogation. Periods of detention in such
cases before the detainee is brought before a judge may last three or four weeks
or longer (as explained later in this chapter, the maximum term should be ten
days under the law). In 1986 and 1987, some human rights activists were
detained in Villa Marista for periods ranging from five to eight months. Earlier
in the 1980s, some *plantados*, were detained for periods of up to two years at
Villa Marista where they completed their prison sentences.[2]

Recently, however, in what Cuban human rights activists have
described as an attempt to appear to reduce the country's political prisoner
population, the authorities have begun to charge their political critics with common crimes, such as contempt, public disorder, or resistance (see Chapter 1,
"Freedom of Expression"). In these cases, detainees are often held before trial
in ordinary police stations. Unfortunately, we have little information about conditions and treatment of such political detainees in police stations. However,
according to one source, Guillermo Rivas Díaz (see Chapter 2, "Freedom of
Association and Assembly"), who was held for two hours in a police station in
Guanabacoa in November 1988, conditions were unpleasant. He was held in a

---

2   Among others, Silvino Rodríguez Barrientos, a former plantado who spent 22 years in
     prison, was held in state security facilities for almost two years between 1983-1985. Accord-
     ing to Rodríguez, psychological pressure is the tool of state security police. He received no
     visits and no correspondence; he was believed to have been "disappeared" by his family and
     friends during this time. Rodríguez was denied medical attention for a time and was forced
     to burst abcesses in his mouth with his fingernails. He was held in a windowless cell and was
     deprived of sleep. Rodríguez was physically beaten once at the beginning of his confinement
     by state security.

cell that measured about 5 x 6 meters with three other detainees. It was dark; there was no window and no light except for the artificial light in the corridor that entered through a space at the top of the solid door. There was a stench. The toilet was a hole in the floor; the shower, a tube in the wall; the water controlled by the police. There were about 12 concrete slab beds, arranged in pairs, one above the other. The beds had foul-smelling, slim mattresses. Rivas Díaz was not physically mistreated while in detention.

In certain cases, detainees are transferred from the G-2 to a pre-trial detention center, the best known of which is La Cabaña which has also been used as a prison. According to Pedro Pablo Sosa, a former political prisoner held there from August 27, 1987 to January 21, 1988 (See Chapter 3, "Freedom of Movement") conditions at La Cabaña were poor. Sosa, who was 20 years old at the time, was held in a galley that housed more than 100 inmates -- juvenile offenders charged with common crimes -- with a window at one end through which fresh air entered the cell. Medical attention and medicines were in short supply. Sosa received visits once a month, and was permitted to have a package brought to him every other month. He had access to the patio for sun once a week for about one hour.

Detention procedures are outlined in the Law of Criminal Procedure, Articles 241 to 244. According to these provisions, anyone may detain a person: who intends to commit a crime when the crime is about to be committed; who is *delincuente in fraganti* (caught in the act of committing the crime); who has escaped from official custody in prison or detention; or the *acusado declarado en rebeldía* (who has been declared absconded). The detention must be reported immediately to the police. An authority or police officer must detain a person in any of the cases mentioned above; when it is a crime against the security of the state; when the crime is punishable by more than six years deprivation of liberty; in cases in which the crime causes alarm or has been frequently committed in the area; or in cases in which there is reason to believe the person would try to evade legal action.

According to Article 245, the police may not hold a detainee for more than 24 hours without informing the investigating officer, who in turn has the next 72 hours to release the detainee or place him at the disposal of the

77

prosecutor. The prosecutor then has the next 72 hours to determine whether to continue to detain, imprison, or release the detainee, or to recommend another precautionary measure. If the prosecutor orders provisional imprisonment or another precautionary measure, he must submit his rationale to the court, which has 72 hours to ratify or vacate the measure, or to substitute another measure. Finally, the detainee is notified of the decision of the Court and is informed of his right to counsel (Article 247). At this point, the detainee may present evidence on his own behalf. Assuming compliance with procedures, detainees may be held for ten days without access to a judge, family members, or counsel, or anyone else of the detainee's choosing. Moreover, under Article 249, in some cases the detainee and defense counsel may be excluded from the investigation until the trial for reasons of state security. Some detainees have been allowed a visit with family members after about one week in detention, however.

Provisional imprisonment must be served in a facility other than a place in which one serves a sentence of deprivation of liberty (Article 251). Alternatives include *fianza en efectivo* (posting bond); *fianza moral*, free on the recognizance of one's employer; house arrest; or periodic appearance before an authority. Suspects in crimes against the security of the state and crimes punishable by death or the maximum prison sentence are excluded from provisional liberty *bajo fianza* (provisional liberty on bond).

Americas Watch believes that arrests should be made only when authorized by judges or magistrates except *in flagrante delicto* and in hot pursuit. In the limited cases in which arrest without warrant is acceptable, a judge should be apprised of the arrest within 24 hours. Judges should be responsible for the detention and for the conditions of detention. Incommunicado detention should be an exceptional measure and must be ordered by a judge, and the reasons must be given. A defendant is entitled to recourse to a competent court to decide without delay on the lawfulness of his arrest or detention and to order his release if the arrest or detention is unlawful.

Prison Conditions

Prison conditions and political imprisonment have long been the focus of human rights attention to Cuba. Since the early 1980s, the accumulation of testimony by Castro's political opponents emerging after twenty years or more of imprisonment has left little doubt that the prisoners were subjected to cruel and degrading treatment in extremely harsh conditions over extraordinarily long periods of time. Confinement either in overcrowded dormitories or in isolation cells; years without contact with visitors; physically debilitating hard labor; beatings and bayonettings by guards; sub-standard or insufficient food; and the withholding of medical attention were among the most reprehensible features of imprisonment in Cuba in the past. Jorge Valls's prison memoir, *Twenty Years and Forty Days: Life in a Cuban Prison*, published in April 1986 by Americas Watch, is an eloquent account of his experience from 1964 to 1984. For a more detailed discussion of current prison conditions in Cuba, see Aryeh Neier's account, "In Cuban Prisons," which appeared in *The New York Review of Books*, on June 30, 1988.

Valls was one of the *plantados*, who refused to participate in the prison "reeducation plan" on political grounds. The *plantados* were arrested during the early years of the Castro regime for their armed and unarmed opposition to the new government. In many cases, it appeared that non-violent opposition to the government was considered to be as serious a crime as armed insurrection. They were held for long periods without trial and then tried before military courts, known as Revolutionary Tribunals, without any semblance of due process. They were sentenced to prison terms generally ranging from twenty to thirty years.

Because they considered themselves political prisoners, the *plantados* resisted "reeducation" by prison authorities by refusing to wear the uniform of those who accept the "plan," which was the uniform of common prisoners; refusing to work; and maintaining a politically antagonistic attitude toward their jailers. Consequently, the *plantados* were denied the benefits of the "plan" such as more food, visits, exercise, and better living conditions. Instead they spent their prison terms wearing underwear, pajamas, or nothing at all. They engaged in hunger strikes and other forms of non-violent protest. And they were punished for their defiant behavior: visits, correspondence, books, and access to outdoors were suspended; their belongings were confiscated during the countless and often violent "inspections" (*requisas*); they were moved to tiny, dark punishment cells and held in isolation.

The *plantados* continue to be mistreated. As recently as May 30, 1988, when prison officials realized that the *plantados* had discovered microphones hidden in their cells, the *plantados* were forcibly taken to the prison hospital and subjected to body searches, X-rays and some were forced to take laxatives by prison officials trying to retrieve the microphones. Those who resisted were beaten and moved to renovated cells in another building where they staged a hunger strike after two were sent to punishment cells in the "rectangle of death" (see below). The *plantados*, whose number had dwindled to 44 at the time, were also protesting being moved to the spruced up cells in what they believed was an effort to mislead the International Committee of the Red Cross and U.N. delegations which were due to examine prison conditions in 1988 for the first time. The two *plantados* in the "rectangle of death" were released after six days and the hunger strike stopped.

Alberto Fibla González, a medical doctor who spent 26 years in prison and now lives in the U.S., diagnosed the 68 *plantados* still in prison earlier in 1988 (all were confined at the same prison, Combinado del Este, near Havana), including himself. He found that 90% of them suffered from physical ailments such as joint disease, prostatitis, hemorrhoids and ulcers that naturally develop as a result of sleeping on damp floors, poor diet and tension for extended periods. Many had deteriorated eyesight from years of inadequate lighting. Some suffered from other serious medical problems such as diabetes and kidney stones.

A decade ago, in 1979, some 400 to 500 *plantados* were in the Cuban prisons, about half of whom were released that year on the condition that they emigrate immediately to the U.S. in accordance with an agreement between the

Carter Administration and the Castro government. In 1986, approximately 126 *plantados* were still serving their sentences[1] ; in 1987, some 80 remained; and in early 1988, approximately 68 were still held. At this writing, four or five remain, though the Cuban government promised early in January 1988 that they would all soon be released -- again, on the condition that they emigrate to the U.S.

According to Cuban prison regulations, under the "reeducation plan" today, prisoners may work for a salary[2] ; continue or complete their schooling to the 9th grade; and receive technical training in practical skills. In addition, in exchange for "political and ideological training," and abiding by prison discipline regulations such as maintaining proper personal appearance, keeping the facilities clean and in order, and standing at attention and showing respect for prison authorities, prisoners are entitled to a number of privileges depending on whether they are repeat offenders or have committed serious crimes or petty crimes. They may have their sentences reduced by up to two months per year; or be released after serving one-third, one-half or two-thirds of their sentence depending on age and conduct. They may receive increased family visits and their families may bring them up to twenty pounds of articles on each visit; and mail privileges.

Americas Watch strongly objects to the political training aspect of the penal program. To seek to change or control the political or ideological beliefs of prisoners is entirely inappropriate particularly in circumstances where privileges are withheld from those who resist. In providing the opportunity for remunerated employment, the Cuban penal program is positive insofar as its

---

1   Valls, Jorge, Twenty Years and Forty Days: Life in a Cuban Prison, Americas Watch, 1986. See Appendix A.

2   Salaries comparable to those paid to non-prisoners for similar work have been paid since 1971. Reductions for the cost of confinement now amount to 35% of the first 100 pesos salary each month; and fifty percent of anything above that. Prisoners whose sentences include fines may have additional deductions to pay off those fines. Despite these deductions, most prisoners keep enough to send regular support payments to their families or to accumulate significant savings.

participants are common criminals or those imprisoned for violent offenses. However, since the Cuban penal system includes inmates imprisoned for peaceful expression or non-violent attempts to leave the country who should not be in prison in the first place, any attempt to condition benefits on their participation in a rehabilitation plan is highly offensive. It is also offensive to deny any prisoner, violent or non-violent, political or non-political, minimally acceptable conditions of confinement as a way of coercing their participation in a rehabilitation plan. Americas Watch does not object to incentives that would attract prisoners to join a rehabilitation plan, as long as it is clear that refusal does not jeopardize the enjoyment of minimal acceptable standards of confinement. We are deeply concerned about the harsh punishment meted out to those prisoners who resist "reeducation."

A new generation of *plantados*, the *nuevos plantados*, or new *plantados*, imprisoned in the late 1970s or early 1980s, have assumed the same defiant posture as their predecessors. They are younger and were sentenced to terms of 5 to 30 years on charges ranging from enemy propaganda to espionage and rebellion. There are believed to be some 20 *nuevos plantados* in Combinado del Este prison. Many have been held in punishment cells for prolonged periods for their refusal to participate in the reeducation plan.

On the grounds of Combinado del Este prison there is a separate building that holds 99 punishment cells, known by prisoners as the "rectangle of death." The cells are about four feet wide and nine or ten feet long. Some can hold up to three prisoners in triple bunk beds. The toilet is a hole in the floor in the back of the cell. The cells were built with double doors: the internal door consists of metal bars partly covered by sheet metal; about two feet in front of the bars is a wooden door that opens onto the corridor. When the outer door is closed, natural light is blocked from entering the cell. A dim electric light bulb controlled by the guards is the only source of light. When representatives of Americas Watch visited the "rectangle of death" in February 1988, most of the outer doors had been removed from the hinges. One of the outer doors that was left in place, when opened, revealed a pitch-dark cell, the inner door of which was solid metal, entirely shutting out all light and ventilation. A small slot at about eye-level, through which food was given to the prisoner, would allow in light only if the outer door is opened. We were told by guards that the prisoner being held there at the time, had no clothes on. Another representative of Americas Watch saw similar conditions a few weeks later at Boniato, Kilo 7 and Nieves Morejon prisons.

Jacinto Fernández González, a *nuevo plantado*, was held in a dark cell in Combinado del Este, sleeping on the floor and naked in the "rectangle of death" for 37 months between 1981-1985. Fernández was sentenced to twenty years in prison in 1981, on charges of espionage. Fernández is said to have submitted statements to the Embassy of Venezuela denouncing human rights violations.

Ariel Hidalgo Guillén, (See Chapter 1, "Freedom of Expression") a member of CCPDH in Combinado del Este, was held in the "rectangle of death" for staging hunger strikes at least twice in the last two years of his imprisonment. Hidalgo, who was released from prison in August 1988, began a hunger strike on September 24, 1986 to protest the persecution of Ricardo Bofill who sought refuge in the French Embassy in Havana in August 1986. On October 3, he was taken to the "rectangle of death," his clothes were taken away, and his water was cut off.

On December 10, 1987, Human Rights Day, Hidalgo offered his food to common prisoners, effectively staging a hunger strike. He felt that the food rations for common prisoners were less adequate than for the political prisoners. Hidalgo was also protesting the treatment of another political prisoner on hunger strike, whose water was cut off. Hidalgo was again taken to the "rectangle of death," where he was left without his clothes and his head was shaved.

Two other *nuevos plantados*, Rodolfo Frómeta Caballero and Angel Donato Martínez García were moved to the "rectangle of death" around the time of the U.N. Commission's visit in September, and were said to remain there at the end of December 1988, on reduced rations of food.

In addition to those in Combinado del Este, punishment cells in three other Cuban prisons were found to be intolerable. Boniato prison in Santiago de Cuba; Kilo 7 prison in Camaguey; and Nieves Morejon in Sancti Spiritus. Punishment cells in Boniato are located in "Boniatico," the prison within the prison, and "4C." They are described in Aryeh Neier's article for *The New York Review of Books*,

> Until a year or two ago, when these cells were primarily used to confine non-violent dissenters and other prisoners held for political offenses, the only opening to the corridors was a four-inch space at the bottom of the door, through which food could be passed. When I visited, these openings were closed and food was handed through the space at the top. The opening at the top is a small improvement: the prisoners need not crouch or lie on the floor to look out and a little more light gets in from the corridors. Some natural light is available in the cells in Boniatico in the daytime through a foot-square barred window without glass, but they lack electric lights. In the generally warm climate of Santiago, these cells must be stiflingly hot. When the weather is cool, as it was during our visit, the cells must be very cold at night....
>
> As bad as the cells were in Boniatico, they were worse in the punishment section of the Boniato prison, 4C. In this cell block, as in cell blocks at two other prisons I saw, prisoners had only bare cement slabs to sleep on; there was no bedding.

Fernando Villalón Moreira (see Chapter 1, "Freedom of Expression") was held in a 4C punishment cell for four months from March to June 1987 for attempting to assert his status as a political prisoner. Americas Watch learned that he was moved there again for some time in the spring of 1988. The reason was that Villalón went on hunger strike to protest his continuing confinement with common prisoners when most, if not all, of the remaining prisoners in Boniato convicted of crimes considered political by the government had been released or transferred to Combinado del Este in May 1988. (See also Appendix B, "Other Cases of Special Concern.")

Neier goes on to describe the facilities at Kilo 7,

> the sixteen punishment cells I saw measured five feet by seven feet and held three prisoners each on three slabs, with a few half-dollar-sized holes in a steel door to admit a tiny amount of electric light from the corridor. There was no natural light. The toilet is a hole in the ground; a spigot provides cold water to flush, to bathe with, and to drink; and the meals consist of

a sparse breakfast and one other meal a day. Prisoners told me that they had been confined naked in such cells.

The Association of the Bar of the City of New York and the Institute for Policy Studies delegations encountered a number of complaints of beatings with rubber hoses, sticks, fists and kicks in Boniato and Combinado del Este. Americas Watch received information abour the kicking to death by guards of Ramón Lance Ortega, a common prisoner, in Combinado del Este in March 1987. The Cuban government has denied this report, claiming that Lance has been released from prison. We have been unable to verify the circumstances of this incident. Repeated efforts by human rights activists to locate and speak with Lance have failed.

Americas Watch has obtained recent information on the treatment of political prisoners convicted of common crimes from Guillermo Rivas Díaz, who was released in January and is now in the United States (see Chapter 2, "Freedom of Association and Assembly"). On the one hand, the cells in which he was confined were harsh; on the other hand, he received certain privileges. Rivas Díaz was held in Combinado del Este prison, the first night, November 29, 1988, with about eight others in a very dark cell, which allowed in light only through the bottom of a solid door. The second day, he was transferred to Guanajay prison in Havana province, where he was held with common prisoners. Almost two weeks later, he was transferred again, this time to Melena-2 prison in Havana province, where he was held in a punishment cell, apparently in reprisal for going on hunger strike in Guanajay prison. He was not permitted to leave the cell during the two weeks of his confinement there, except on one occasion: he was permitted an overnight conjugal visit with his wife in the women's prison. There is reason to suspect that he was granted the privilege of a conjugal visit after only about one month in prison, because he was soon to be released along with his father.

According to Aimee Llado, Rivas Díaz's wife, who is also now in the U.S., her confinement in the women's prison outside Havana, the *Centro de Reeducación de Mujeres de Occidente*, was not as difficult. She was denied dental attention, but otherwise had no complaints of mistreatment. She was permitted the conjugal visit with her husband. Llado was held with common prisoners, although she was able to see her mother-in-law and another political prisoner, Rita Fleitas. In the women's prison the political prisoners are not held together, but rather dispersed among the common prisoners, so that there is no cohesive political prisoner community. She learned that there were a number of political prisoners convicted on technically common crimes, such as contempt.

Llado noted that the prisoners were expected to keep the facilities in perfect order for all the visitors who pass through the prison, and therefore, conditions were clean and orderly. Her account concurred with the impressions of Americas Watch representatives from visits to the prison in February and March. In fact, although Americas Watch has received reports that there have been problems such as water leaks and insect infestation in the past, today the women's prison is a model prison, a show place. It is the prison most frequently seen by visitors to Cuba's prisons.

Americas Watch remains concerned, however, about the Cuban government's on-going practice of imprisoning its critics, and is disturbed that even in a model prison such as the women's prison, with excellent medical facilities, medical attention requested by a prisoner was denied.

Nevertheless, despite persistent reports of beatings and harsh punishment in some of Cuba's prisons, conditions of confinement are substantially less bad today than during the first twenty-five years of the revolution. Recent changes, such as increased visits and correspondence, as well as renovations of parts of several prison buildings, are commendable. We believe increased attention and access to the prisons by foreign visitors has had a very salutory effect.

Psychiatric Confinement

Americas Watch is concerned about reports of the confinement of political prisoners in psychiatric hospitals, or the abuse of psychiatry by Cuban authorities to silence their opponents.

Nicolas Guillén Landrian, a former filmmaker, artist and poet, was expelled from ICAIC, the national film institute, in 1973 after his films were found to be "incoherent" or inconsistent with the goals of the revolution. One film, *Cof-*

fea Arabiga, a 20-minute documentary on an agricultural plan implemented at the time, contained a scene in which Fidel Castro is seen climbing a mountain to the background soundtrack of the Beatles' "Fool on the Hill." He had also refused to participate in an ICAIC film made in an effort to discredit Cuban writer Heberto Padilla who held "counterrevolutionary attitudes."

Guillén worked in a construction job until 1976 when he was arrested and accused of attempting to assassinate Castro. The charge was reportedly based on a comment he made at a social gathering. This charge was not pursued. However, he was held for six months without trial in the state security facility Villa Marista, and was interrogated but not physically abused. At his 1977 trial, he was sentenced to two years for "ideological diversionism."

During his imprisonment in Combinado del Este prison, he was taken to both the prison hospital and to the Havana Psychiatric Hospital and submitted to electric shock treatment. He was later returned to Combinado del Este until his release. Guillén was released in 1979 only to be arrested six months later on two counts of "dangerousness," (see Chapter 4, "Privacy and Surveillance") and served four more years.

He is now living in his home in Havana and is a member of the Cuban Committee for Human Rights.

In July 1988, Jesus Leyva Guerra, a human rights activist, was detained and, at this writing, continues to be held in a psychiatric hospital in Santiago de Cuba (see Chapter 2, "Freedom of Association and Assembly"). Leyva is reported to have been subjected to a series electric shock treatments, and was unable to recognize his wife on a recent visit.[3]

Americas Watch has reason to believe Leyva has been confined to a psychiatric hospital as a reprisal for his human rights activity. Nevertheless, the details of his case remain unclear. If Leyva has been confined to treat any men-

---

3   See Schanche, Don A., "Cuban Rights Crackdown, Psychiatric Abuses Told," The Los Angeles Times, January 12, 1988. See also Treaster, Joseph B., "Cuban Rights: Even Today Not So Libre," The New York Times, Januar 19, 1989.

tal illness he may suffer, why has he been held in the judicial ward of the hospital? If he has been held in the judicial ward because he has criminal charges pending against him, what are they? If it is because he is considered by judicial authorities to be dangerous to himself or to society, has he actually caused harm to himself or to another person, or is this a form of preventive detention?

While the abuse of psychiatry for political purposes is not known to be widespread in Cuba, Americas Watch has learned that a number of prisoners of conscience have been held in psychiatric hospitals during the initial period of detention, ostensibly to diagnose the prisoners' mental health. The following two prisoners of conscience recently released from Combinado del Este prison, were confined in the Havana Psychiatric Hospital upon arrest on charges of "enemy propaganda."

Ariel Hidalgo Guillen (see Chapter 1, "Freedom of Expression") spent the first twenty days of his detention in Villa Marista, and then was transferred to the psychiatric hospital. According to Hidalgo, he was held in a room with approximately one hundred criminally psychotic patients for ten days. No physicians or guards visited the ward during the time he was there. He had difficulty sleeping for fear of being attacked while he slept.

Julio Vento Roberes, a musician and cartoonist, was arrested in 1977 for drawing anti-government caricatures, and was reportedly confined in a psychiatric hospital for five years. Vento, who is 56 years old, began drawing cartoons again after his release. He was rearrested in 1982 and sentenced to eight years, again on charges of "enemy propaganda." Vento was previously imprisoned in 1960.

AIDS

It has not been customary to discuss a nation's practices with respect to those infected with the AIDS virus in human rights reports. Inevitably, however, this will change as the disease spreads and as the practices of governments raise questions involving such matters as freedom of expression, freedom of information and, as in Cuba, liberty itself.

To our knowledge, Cuba is the only nation in the world that confines all those identified as HIV carriers, that is those who test positive as carriers of the AIDS virus. It is also, so far as we know, the only nation that has ordered universal testing to determine whether its citizens have become infected by the virus.[1] In the course of a television program broadcast on October 25, 1988 on the Cuban government's Tele-Rebelde Network, Dr. Hector Terry Molinet, Vice Minister of Public Health, reported that from the time testing began in February 1986 until October 20, 1988, the government had tested 2,956,144 Cubans (out of a population of some ten million); and that 259 had tested positive, of whom 188 were males and 71 were females.[2]

According to Terry:

Cuba's strategy for fighting the Acquired Immunodeficiency Syndrome is predicated on four basic principles. The first one is the massive detection of carriers through massive screenings of large population groups. This also includes screening

---

1   Though Americas Watch is not aware of other nations that have adopted such policies, they have been proposed elsewhere. For example, the French neo-fascist leader Jean-Marie Le Pen has called for mandatory testing and quarantine in France.

2   A transcript of the program, translated into English, was published by the Foreign Broadcast Information Service, LAT-88-208, on October 27, 1988 at pp. 2-8.

blood donations. Second, the epidemiological study of each of the carriers detected so that we can quickly detect others who have been affected through sexual contacts with the carriers. Third, treatment in a regimented sanatorium to prevent the spread of the disease and to give better treatment to AIDS carriers. Finally, and a very important principle under which we are holding this program tonight, is to maintain the most detailed and periodic dissemination of information so that the population knows how to prevent and avoid contamination.

It should be noted that Cuba is not one of the nations that has been particularly hard hit by AIDS. Accordingly, mandatory testing and the confinement of all those testing positive are not reactions to an actual national emergency. Accepting the Cuban government's figures on the number of those testing positive -- that is fewer than one in ten thousand of those tested -- the incidence is far lower than in many other countries, including than in the United States. Rather, the denial of liberty to those testing positive in Cuba is described by Cuban officials as a preventive measure. As Dr. Terry said on the Tele-Rebelde program, "If we had followed procedures established in other countries which differ from our strategy, we would probably now have 4,000 people" who tested positive. Whether or not the program is successful at keeping AIDS in check, Americas Watch is concerned with the civil liberties issues involved. Moreover, Cuba has not demonstrated that programs that restrict civil liberties less drastically are ineffectual.

The Tele-Rebelde program also broadcast pictures of the Santiago de Las Vegas sanatorium where those testing positive are confined. Lucia González, the program's host, described these as "truly beautiful pictures" showing "a pleasant place." An American who visited in October 1988, Dr. Ronald Bayer, Associate Professor at Columbia University's School of Public Health, said the facility "was neither barracks-like nor dungeon-like, although I have to assume we were shown the best." Bayer described what he saw as resembling typical Cuban suburban apartments. "They were modestly furnished, and the common living room in each apartment had a large TV set. In one, there was a big picture of Che." Bayer also spoke to several detainees. "One couldn't expect candor," he reported. "Our conversations took place in the presence of the head of the sanatorium and half of the staff. One person said he felt he was doing his best to defend the Cuban revolution."[3]

Though confinement of those testing positive is for life, at least some -- and perhaps all -- are periodically permitted to leave the sanatorium. Dr. Manuel Hernández Liens, a Cuban health official who directs the Sanatorium stated on the Tele-Rebelde program that:

> We have established a pass system for Havana patients who go out every Sunday and for patients from the interior who, because of distance, are given a 4-day pass every 45 days. This pass does not include transportation to their province. The patient is accompanied by a health worker, a technician or a professional that is trained in the responsibilities of caring for this person during his leave. These measures are an attempt to prevent, at any cost, the patient from having sexual relations with his partner or from having an occasional contact among the population. The pass system for the sanatorium patients is in force under these conditions.

In the sanatorium there are reportedly 20 or 25 married couples. Dr. Hernández asserted that:

> life in the institution is very full in the sense that they have opportunities to work. They can participate in sports. Some of them are members of a musical group which was recently created. We are creating certain conditions.

> Courses were recently approved for patients who interrupted their university studies. We are coordinating this with the Ministry of Higher Education so that many of them can take free tests and get their degrees. They participate in sports. They have opportunities to work.

> All this is optional. The patient is not required at any time to work, study or do anything else.

---

3   Victor F. Zonana, "Cuba's AIDS Quarantine Center Called Frightening," Los Angeles Times, November 4, 1988.

Though the Tele-Rebelde broadcast was not wholly explicit in discussing the compulsory aspects of confinement of those testing positive, an exchange near the end of the program was revealing. Lucia González, the host, asked:

> Some of our callers have spoken about patients who have escaped from the sanatorium. What happens to that patient? Have there been such cases of patients and carriers escaping?

Dr. Hernández responded:

> First of all, the sanatorium is a health institute. It is not a prison. We saw pictures of it earlier. People occasionally escape from the most secure prisons. The sanatorium is not exempt from the possibility that a patient, a carrier, could violate the disciplinary measures.

> As was mentioned earlier, once the patient is admitted, he is briefed extensively on the operations of the sanatorium. This is one of the measures that is insisted upon. They are told they can only go out with their companion when they have a pass or if they have a social problem or if the patient has some other type of need.

González persisted: "Do you punish the patients that escape?" Hernández responded that: "We call attention to this problem; we meet with him, etc."

Cuba's method of dealing with those carrying the AIDS virus raises a critical question: is it permissible to deprive some persons of liberty in order to protect others? Phrased in such a broad way, of course, the answer must be yes. All would agree, for example, that a murderer may be deprived of freedom to punish him and to protect the innocent. It is when the question is refined, however, that answering it becomes more complicated. What if the person who poses a threat, unlike the murderer, is not at fault, and does not deserve punishment, but is himself the victim of something beyond his control? What if we are not certain that a person poses a threat? What if the person is not at fault, and it is possible to reduce or minimize any potential threat by means that do not involve the deprivation of liberty? Or by means that do not deprive the person of liberty so drastically as in Cuba?

It is not surprising that a government that makes *peligrosidad* (dangerousness) punishable by confinement would also confine those who test

HIV positive. Cuba has chosen to eliminate all risks posed by a group of its citizens who have not been found guilty of any offense by completely depriving them of liberty. It is an approach that, we believe, reflects the relative weight given to security and to liberty by the Cuban government.

United States Policy

Particularly during the past two years, the United States has engaged in a campaign to denounce abuses of human rights in Cuba. This has had a salutory impact in helping to focus international attention on long-standing abuses; regrettably, because the campaign has been marked by greatly exaggerated charges and a high level of politicization, it has also done damage to the human rights cause generally and could ultimately backfire insofar as Cuba itself is concerned.

Speaking at the United Nations Commission on Human Rights in Geneva in March 1987, U.S. Ambassador to the United Nations Vernon Walters denounced Cuba for continuing to hold "15,000 or more" political prisoners. However the term "political prisoner" is defined -- that is, whether the term is only applied to those imprisoned in reprisal for peaceful expression and association and for non-violent attempts to leave the country, or whether it also is applied to those imprisoned for politically motivated violence -- Ambassador Walters's charge bore no relation to reality. Yet in an apparent effort to buttress Walters's charge, the State Department cited an estimate of 15,500 political prisoners in its *Country Reports* for 1987, published in February 1988.[1] The *Country Reports* also cited "numerous incidents of torture"; "disappearances";

---

1   In January 1989, a Miami-based, Spanish-language newspaper published statements by former long-time prisoner Armando Valladares, the head of the U.S. delegation to the UNCHR in 1988 and possibly in 1989. Included in his statements which were meant to discredit a human rights activist in Cuba, Valladares put the current number of political prisoners at close to 10,000. He used this figure to refute a recent statement by the human rights activist in Cuba that the number of political prisoners, including conscientious objectors and those convicted of attempting to leave the country illegally, is 600 or 700. Whether

and some 17 political executions at Combinado del Este prison between July 1986 and June 1987. Our own investigations indicate that these charges are without basis.

In March 1987, a U.S. effort to secure adoption of a resolution condemning Cuba for "massive, systematic, and flagrant abuses of human rights" was defeated by a vote of 19-18. In March 1988, however, a close vote was avoided on a similar but more restrained U.S. resolution when a compromise by several Latin American governments was accepted by the Cubans and ultimately by the UNCHR as a whole. Under the compromise, the Cuban government invited the UNCHR to send a delegation to Cuba to conduct a human rights investigation. The heightened scrutiny had a beneficial impact on Cuban human rights practices, as a few hundred prisoners held for politically motivated offenses were released in anticipation of both the UNCHR vote and the delegation's visit.

Though the United States was responsible for securing the debate at the United Nations which resulted in the UNCHR visit, and the consequences of that debate and visit were good for the cause of human rights in Cuba, we remain apprehensive that the effort might backfire. We assume that the U.N. delegation will find the charges of torture, disappearances, political executions and the charge of 10,000 or 15,000 political prisoners to be baseless. This could create the impression that there is not a serious human rights problem in Cuba. As we have attempted to demonstrate in this report, it would be very unfortunate if the international community were to be left with that impression.

---

the figure of 10,000 is Valladares's personal count or that of the Department of State, Americas Watch considers it to be a gross exaggeration. (Also not explained is the change from Ambassador Walters's "more than 15,000" in 1987 to Valladares's "close to 10,000" in 1989. A few hundred prisoners held for politically motivated offenses are known to have been released, not 5,000.) Moreover, Americas Watch considers Valladares's statements attacking a human rights monitor in Cuba to be not constructive in promoting the cause of human rights in Cuba.

Denials of freedom of expression, freedom of assembly, privacy, due process of law and freedom of movement are not so sensational as torture, disappearances, political executions and massive political imprisonment. Yet these denials of human rights in Cuba are so pervasive as to make the human rights situation very poor even after the remaining political prisoners are released. It would be unfortunate if international attention to abuses of human rights were to dissipate if the Cuban government succeeds in rebutting baseless charges by the United States. It is for this reason that we believe that, though the United States performed a valuable service by focusing international attention on the human rights situation in Cuba, in the long run it may have done a disservice to the cause of improving that situation.

Americas Watch also objects to the role of the Department of State in discouraging international inspections of prison conditions by private groups by refusing to issue visas to Cubans to inspect U.S. prisons after a group of Americans inspected Cuban prisons. Several persons associated with Americas Watch had taken part in visits to six Cuban prisons in February and March 1988 organized by the Institute for Policy Studies, and had been able to interview more than 120 Cuban prisoners of their choice outside the presence of Cuban authorities. Four Cubans sought visas to the U.S. to conduct similar prison visits here, and all the public prisons they wished to visit expressed willingness to allow them to do so. Even so, the State Department blocked the visit by the Cubans. The State Department action already has had the unfortunate consequence of interfering with visits by a U.S. human rights group to the Czech prisons because the Czechs objected to the denial of reciprocal visits in the case of the Cubans. Exchange visits to prisons are of potentially great value in spotlighting abuses in prisons and in gathering information on prisoners. It is Americas Watch's hope that the Bush Administration will play a more constructive role in this regard than the Reagan Administration.

The Reagan Administration played a more positive role in its final year in certain other respects. Pursuant to an immigration agreement reinstated in November 1987, about 2,500 political prisoners, former political prisoners and family members from Cuba entered the United States with refugee status an important humanitarian contribution that belatedly fulfills a 1980 pledge by the

U.S. Interests Section in Havana under the Carter Administration. Previously, those persons were the innocent victims of a dispute between Cuba and the U.S. over Cuba's refusal to take back the excludable aliens who came to the U.S. during the Mariel boatlift. (A previous period during which visas were issued in late 1984 and early 1985 came to an end when Fidel Castro suspended an immigration agreement in anger over the launching of Radio Martí in May 1985.)

Also, in August 1988, the Reagan Administration endorsed a trade bill that lifts restrictions on Cuban books, films and records, easing a 27-year-old trade embargo, which in earlier years, the Administration had made more rigid. Increasing the free flow of information and ideas, we believe, is a contribution to the protection of human rights.

APPENDIX A
THE PERSECUTION OF HUMAN RIGHTS MONITORS[1]

Enrique Acosta Ruiz was briefly detained in September in connection with his attempt to meet with a delegation of the UN Commission on Human Rights.[2]

Raúl Alemán Valdez was briefly detained in September in connection with his attempt to meet with a delegation of the UN Commission on Human Rights (see footnote).

José Luis Alvarado Delgado (see the 1987 report), who had last been imprisoned in August 1986, was released from Combinado del Este prison on

---

1   From The Persecution of Human Rights Monitors, December 1987 to December 1988, A Worldwide Survey, December 1988, Human Rights Watch.

2   The UN delegation, which was conducting a human rights investigation from September 16 to 25, arranged for Cubans who wanted to raise their cases or report human rights abuses to go to the Hotel Comodoro in Havana. During the week of September 19, two incidents that occurred in front of the hotel resulted in the arrest of an unknown number of persons. On September 19, when the UN delegation returned from an appointment outside the hotel, the crowd of people waiting to see them broke into applause and cheers. After the delegation entered the hotel, the police arrested a number of people, took them to the Villa Marista state security facility, fined them, and eventually released them. On September 21, the police stationed in front of the hotel had been harassing some of those waiting to meet with the delegation and reportedly prevented or threatened to prevent some of those individuals from entering the hotel. An undetermined number of people are believed to have been detained at that time. Some of those detained that week were held for several hours, others for several days. Still others were reportedly arrested or rearrested and held for varying lengths of time after the UN delegation left Cuba. At this writing it remains unclear exactly when and under what circumstances Acosta and others listed below were arrested.

March 19 and seeks to emigrate from Cuba. On October 12 he was denied permission to leave the country.

Alberto Anaya was briefly detained in September in connection with his attempt to meet with a delegation of the UN Commission on Human Rights (see footnote).

Armando Araya García, affiliated with "Pro Arte Libre,"[3] was arrested on October 20 after gathering with about a dozen other members of the group to place a floral wreath at a monument to José Martí in Havana. They started to read a statement to commemorate the official "Cuban Culture Day," when several dozen people dressed in civilian clothes reportedly approached the PAL group and began to assault them verbally and physically. Uniformed police quickly intervened and arrested six PAL members (see below). None of the attackers was arrested. They were all tried and sentenced on October 24 on charges of "public disorder" (Penal Code Article 200.1). Their sentences were upheld on appeal on November 2. Araya is serving a one-year sentence in 5 1/2 prison in Pinar del Río.

---

3   The "Asociación Pro Arte Libre," — Association for Free Art — a group advocating free expression and freedom of artistic creation, has divided into two sections since its founding in August 1988. For the purpose of clarity, in this report the section led by Pablo Roberto Pupo Sánchez and Juan Enrique García is referred to as "Asociación Pro Arte Libre" (APAL); the group led by Armando Araya Garcia is referred to as "Pro Arte Libre" (PAL); At the time of its founding, the group submitted an application to the Ministry of Justice requesting official recognition as a legal association. It has not received a response from the government at this writing.

Gustavo Arcos Bergnes (see the 1987 report), affiliated with the Cuban Committee for Human Rights (CCPDH),[4] who had been imprisoned since 1981, was released from Combinado del Este prison on March 10. His continuing efforts to emigrate have met with repeated denial of permission to leave the country. His passport was confiscated in July.

Sebastian Arcos Bergnes, affiliated with CCPDH (see footnote), who served six years in prison for attempting to leave the country illegally, was released from Combinado del Este prison on May 4, 1987. Like his brother, he has been repeatedly denied permission to leave the country. Arcos was last denied permission in August.

Alejandro Benítez Ferrer was arrested in September in connection with his attempt to meet with a delegation of the UN Commission on Human Rights (see footnote). He was reportedly charged with either "resistance" (Article 143) or "contempt" (*desacato*, Article 144) and sentenced to three months in prison. He is believed to be serving his term in Combinado del Este prison.

Francisco Benítez Ferrer, who is affiliated with CCPDH, was arrested in September in connection with his attempt to meet with a delegation of the UN Commission on Human Rights (see footnote). He, like his brother, Alejandro Benítez Ferrer, was reportedly charged with either "resistance" or "contempt" and sentenced to six months in prison. He is serving his term in Combinado del Este prison. At the beginning of September, Francisco Benítez had been released early from Combinado del Este prison where he had been held

---

4   The Cuban Committee for Human Rights, which was the first independent organization in Cuba dedicated to monitoring and promoting human rights, was created in 1976 by several people associated with the University of Havana, and others. The Committee was reorganized in 1984 inside the Combinado del Este prison where its main leaders were imprisoned for their dissident activity. CCPDH organized a network of prisoners and ex-prisoners to gather and smuggle out information on political prisoners and on prison conditions. CCPDH remains an illegal organization, despite numerous attempts to register officially. A new group, the Cuban Commission for Human Rights and National Reconciliation (CCDHRN) was formed in October 1987; it is an offshoot of CCPDH, but independent of it.

since December 1986. He was serving a five-year sentence on charges of "enemy propaganda," reportedly for writing quotes from José Martí, Cuba's national hero, on a wall.

Ricardo Bofill Pagés, the President of CCPDH (see footnote), was detained on January 26, along with two other CCPDH members, Rafael Saumell Muñoz and Rolando Cartaya (see below). They were held for several hours for questioning at state security police headquarters on the eve of a human rights press conference they planned to which representatives of various embassies and the press had been invited. On February 17, an independent art exhibit organized by CCPDH was disrupted by a crowd of neighbors that had gathered outside the house, ostensibly spontaneously, to assault those attending the exhibit verbally and physically, including Bofill and many members of CCPDH. The crowd is presumed to have been sponsored by state security police. A few weeks later, Bofill was the subject of numerous virulent attacks in the Cuban media including long articles in the Communist Party paper *Granma*, the humor magazine *Palante*, and a 3-part television series. This attempt to discredit Bofill and CCPDH came one week after the vote in March on Cuba at the UN Commission on Human Rights in Geneva. Reportedly, he has also been subjected to other incidents of extra-legal harassment, such as verbal and physical abuse by unidentified persons, who are presumed to have been state security agents or encouraged by them.

Bofill emigrated to West Germany on October 6 after years of repeatedly being denied permission to leave the country.

Rolando Cartaya, affiliated with CCPDH (see footnote), was detained on January 26 along with Ricardo Bofill Pagés (see Bofill above). Cartaya emigrated to the U.S. in May, after years of repeatedly being denied permission to leave the country.

Domingo Jorge Delgado Fernández (see the 1987 report), a lawyer and member of the CCPDH (see footnote), who had been imprisoned since 1981, was released from Combinado del Este prison on May 9. He remains in Cuba but seeks to emigrate.

Tania Díaz Castro, President of the Cuban Human Rights Party, was arrested on November 29 along with her son, Guillermo Rivas Díaz, and his

102

wife, Aimee Llado Canton, during a visit with Díaz's ex-husband, Guillermo Rivas Porta. Rivas Porta was a political prisoner who served more than 21 years in prison and at the time was being held in Combinado del Este prison. Díaz, Rivas and Llado were arrested, summarily tried and sentenced on the same day to 1 year, 1 year and 3 months, respectively, on charges of "public disorder." Díaz's arrest may be in connection with a Cuban Human Rights Party document released earlier in November calling for a plebiscite and constitutional reform in Cuba. The Cuban Human Rights Party was formed in 1988 by several members of CCPDH. Guillermo Rivas Porta was released on January 3, 1989 along with Guillermo Rivas Diaz and Aimee Llado Canton. They are presently residing in the United States. Tania Diaz Castro is serving her sentence in the women's prison outside Havana.

Rita Fleitas Fernández, who is affiliated with "Pro Arte Libre," was arrested on October 20 (see Araya above). She is serving a nine-month prison term in the Centro de Reeducación de Mujeres del Occidente, the women's prison outside Havana.

Juan Enrique García, who is affiliated with the "Asociación Pro Arte Libre" (see footnote), was arrested on October 18 and is reportedly being held without trial in Villa Marista state security facility.

Vladimir García Alderete, who is affiliated with "Pro Arte Libre," was arrested on October 20 (see Araya above). He is believed to be serving a nine-month prison term in Combinado del Este prison.

Secundino Hernández Castro, who is affiliated with "Pro Arte Libre," was arrested on October 20 (see Araya above). He is believed to be serving a seven-month prison term in Combinado del Este prison.

Ariel Hidalgo Guillén (see the 1987 report), Vice President of the CCPDH (see footnote), who had been imprisoned since 1981, was released from Combinado del Este prison on August 4 and flown directly to the U.S.

David Hornedo García, who is affiliated with "Pro Arte Libre," was arrested on October 20 (see Araya above). He is believed to be serving a seven-month prison term in Combinado del Este prison.

Raúl Leon Godoy (see the 1987 report), who had been imprisoned since 1981, was released from Combinado del Este prison in June 1988.

103

Jesus Leyva Guerra, who reports regularly from Santiago de Cuba to both CCPDH and the Cuban Commission for Human Rights and National Reconciliation (see footnote), was detained by state security police on July 14 and taken to the Gustavo Machín Psychiatric Hospital near Santiago de Cuba. He is reportedly being held in the "pabellón judicial" of the hospital, without charge. There is reason to believe that he may have been placed in psychiatric detention because of his human rights activities as Leyva was reportedly detained at the home of a family he was interviewing in the course of his human rights work.

Lázaro Linares Echevarría was detained in September in connection with his attempt to meet with a delegation of the UN Commission for Human Rights (see footnote). He is reportedly serving a six-month prison sentence on charges of "contempt" in Quivicán prison.

Pablo Llabre Raurell, who is affiliated with CCPDH (see footnote), was subjected to a so-called *acto de repudio* ("act of repudiation") on September 28, the twenty-eighth anniversary of the government-sponsored Committees for the Defense of the Revolution (CDR). Members of the local CDRs, neighborhood surveillance groups, gathered in front of his home in Havana and, using loudspeakers, verbally assaulted Llabre and denounced his participation in CCPDH activities.

León Alex Matos Cabrera, who is affiliated with the "Associación Pro Arte Libre" (see footnote), was arrested some time in late October and is reportedly being held without trial in Villa Marista state security facility.

Rogelio Morto Guerra (see the 1987 report), who had been imprisoned since 1981, was released from Combinado del Este prison in December 1987. He emigrated to the U.S. in April.

Ramón Obregón Sarduy, who is affiliated with the "Asociación Pro Arte Libre" (see footnote), was arrested on October 18 and is reportedly being held without trial in Villa Marista state security facility.

Gilberto Plasencia Jimenez, who is affiliated with the "Asociación Pro Arte Libre" (see footnote), was arrested in late October and is reportedly being held without trial in Villa Marista state security facility.

Pablo Roberto Pupo Sánchez, who is affiliated with the "Asociación Pro Arte Libre" (see footnote), was arrested on October 18 and is reportedly being held without trial in Villa Marista state security facility.

Raul Robaina Renovales (see the 1987 report), who had been imprisoned since 1982, was released from Combinado del Este prison in April. He remains in Cuba and has been subjected to harassment, such as visits to his home by state security police.

Lázaro la Rosa Arbolay was briefly detained in September in connection with his attempt to meet with a delegation of the UN Commission on Human Rights (see footnote).

Elizardo Sánchez Santa Cruz, head of CCDHRN (see footnote), was openly followed by state security agents in September upon return from a three-month visit to the U.S. and during the visit of the UN Commission on Human Rights, with which his group met. In October he was fired from his job at a library in Havana.

Rafael Saumell Muñoz, who was affiliated with CCPDH (see footnote) at the time, was detained on January 26 along with Ricardo Bofill Pagés (see Bofill above). Saumell emigrated to the U.S. in May.

Andrés Solares Teseiro (see the 1987 report), who had been imprisoned since 1981, was released from Combinado del Este prison on May 13, 1988 and flown directly to the U.S.

Aída Valdés Santana, who is affiliated with "Pro Arte Libre," was arrested on October 20 (see Araya above). She is serving seven months house arrest. (Health reasons apparently were responsible for the use of house arrest instead of imprisonment.)

Teodoro del Valle (see the 1987 report), who had been imprisoned since 1980, was released from Combinado del Este prison at the end of 1987. He is currently living in the U.S.

Raúl de la Vega Gómez was briefly detained in September in connection with his attempt to meet with a delegation of the UN Commission on Human Rights (see footnote).

Gustavo Venta was arrested in September in connection with his attempt to meet with a delegation of the UN Commission on Human Rights (see footnote), and sentenced to six months in prison either for "resistance" or "contempt." He is serving his term in Combinado del Este prison.

The following are prisoners who monitor prison conditions and treatment of political prisoners in Combinado del Este. Their confinement or their continuing confinement is not necessarily a result of their human rights activity.

Mario Chanes de Armas (see the 1987 report), who participated in the 1956 Granma landing, was arrested in 1961 after retiring from the armed forces because of his opposition to the new government, and sentenced to 30 years in prison. He is a *plantado*, a long-term political prisoner who has refused "reeducation."

Pedro Jorge Dorta Rodriguez (see the 1987 report), was arrested in 1980 and charged with rebellion for his association with a group trying to organize a political movement, and sentenced to 15 years in prison. Another person arrested in connection with this case reportedly died in detention.

Jacinto Fernandez Gonzalez (see the 1987 report), photographer, was arrested in 1981, charged with espionage and sentenced to 20 years. Fernandez submitted statements denouncing human rights violations to the Embassy of Venezuela. He has spent four years in a punishment cell in the "rectangle of death" in Combinado del Este prison.

Samuel Hernandez Reyes (see the 1987 report), was arrested in 1980, charged with violation of the right of extra-territoriality, and sentenced to 25 years for attempting to seek asylum in the Papal nunciature.

Alfredo Jimenez Ramos (see the 1987 report), was arrested in 1980 on the charge of violation of the right of extra-territoriality and sentenced to 25 years for attempting to seek asylum in the Papal nunciature.

Sandor Mendoza Mendoza (see the 1987 report), television director and writer, was arrested in 1983, charged with terrorism and sentenced to 20 years. It is believed he was imprisoned for voicing criticism of the government at work.

106

Roberto del Risco (see the 1987 report), a student, was arrested in 1986 on the charge of espionage and sentenced to seven years. It is believed he was imprisoned for human rights-related activity.

Enrique Ruiz Cabrera (see the 1987 report), 30, was arrested in 1981 on charges of enemy propaganda, attempt to leave the country illegally, and preparing to commit acts that affect the right of extra-territoriality, and sentenced to 10 years. It is believed he was arrested for being in possession of political pamphlets and for his attempts to leave the country.

Omitted from the 1987 report:

Julio Vento Roberes, who was affiliated with CCPDH (see footnote) in Combinado del Este Prison and who had been arrested in 1983 and sentenced to eight years on charges of "enemy propaganda," was released from Combinado del Este prison in August and flown directly to the U.S.

APPENDIX B
OTHER CASES OF SPECIAL CONCERN TO
AMERICAS WATCH

Amado Rodríguez Fernández, 45, a former long-term political prisoner, is serving a second prison sentence of 15 years on charges of rebellion, enemy propaganda and speculation. Americas Watch has reason to believe he was imprisoned for his writings which were never published but which he produced independently. Rodríguez was arrested in July 1984 and held in "Boniatico," the prison within the prison of Boniato, until March 1988, when he was transferred to Combinado del Este prison, where he has spent much of his time in the hospital.

On December 13, 1988, Rodríguez was forced to put on the uniform of a common prisoner, transferred to Guanajay prison, and confined with a common prisoner. Later he was transferred to a cell by himself and went on hunger strike. On December 29 he was transferred back to the Combinado del Este hospital, where he is believed to be held at this writing.

Rodríguez was first imprisoned in 1961 for belonging to a counter-revolutionary group and sentenced to 30 years. He was one of the "defiant prisoners," known as *plantados*, who rejected the prison re-education plan and other forms of prison discipline. He was released after serving 18 years in prison as part of a large-scale release program (*indulto*) in 1979.

Americas Watch is concerned about the health of Amado Rodríguez, who has spent half his life in prison. We believed Rodríguez has been imprisoned for the peaceful expression of his ideas.

Fernando Villalón Moreira, 27, arrested in 1986 on charges of "contempt," (see Chapter 1, "Freedom of Expression") has been held in Boniato prison with common prisoners, where until February 1988 he was receiving only one visit every six months. More recently he is believed to be receiving one visit every two months.

On May 22, 1988, the 15-20 political prisoners remaining in Boniato prison were transferred to another prison or released. Villalón was left behind because he is considered a common prisoner by authorities. In order to assert his status as a political prisoner, Villalón declared a hunger strike. Soon after, he was transferred to a punishment cell in the prison within Boniato prison, known as "Boniatico," and held there for several days. The cells in Boniatico are tiny and most confine one prisoner each. A four-inch-wide space at the top of the solid iron door allows in light from the hall, and there is a small window without glass that lets in natural light during the day, but there is no electric light in the cell. The cells become very hot during the summer. At this writing, Villalón continues to be held in Boniato.

Villalón was previously imprisoned in May 1980 on charges of "enemy propaganda" for putting up posters, and sentenced to 3 years in prison. He was a *plantado*, serving his sentence with the long-term prisoners who refused to accept the re-education plan. When his term was to be completed in May 1983, he was taken to a state security facility in Santiago, and held there for 47 days, during which he was severely mistreated. He was accused of heading acts of sabotage and propaganda while in prison, and served another year for these alleged infractions (*delito post-delictivo*). He was released in June 1984. Villalón was reportedly one of the prisoners who should have been permitted to emigrate through the efforts of Jesse Jackson at that time.

Americas Watch is disturbed that Fernando Villalón is being held among common prisoners because he is considered a common prisoner by the Cuban authorities. We believe he has been imprisoned for the peaceful expression of his ideas.

Americas Watch is concerned about the plantados who remain in prison at this writing. We welcome the release of most of the long-term prisoners through an agreement between the Cuban government and the U.S. Catholic Conference. We urge the Cuban government to release immediately **Mario Chanes de Armas**, who has served 28 years in prison; **Ernesto Díaz Rodríguez,**

110

20 years; **Alberto Grau Sierra,** 25 years; and **José Mustelier Nuevo,** 20 years. At this writing it is unclear whether Eleno Oviedo Alvarez, who has been imprisoned for 26 years, remains in prison. They are serving lengthy prison sentences after trials that lacked any semblance of due process, and have spent much of their time in prison in extremely harsh conditions.

Copies of this report are available for $10.00 from:

Human Rights Watch

36 West 44th Street	1522 K Street, N.W.
Room 911	Suite 910
New York, NY 10036	Washington, D.C. 20005
212-840-9460	202-371-6592